Breaking
FREE

McDougal & Associates

Servants of Christ and Stewards of the
Mysteries of God

Breaking FREE

A Manual for Finding Deliverance through Prayer and Fasting

by

Jane P. McCoy

Cover image from Shutterstock.com

Published by:

McDougal & Associates
18896 Greenwell Springs Road
Greenwell Springs, LA 70739

www.ThePublishedWord.com

McDougal & Associates is an organization dedicated to the spreading of the Gospel of the Lord Jesus Christ to as many people as possible in the shortest time possible.

ISBN: 978-1-940461-66-3

Printed in the U.S., the U.K. and Australia
For Worldwide Distribution

DEDICATION

First, I want to dedicate this work to the Lord. It was His desire to share this manual with His children, and I thank Him for birthing it. I also thank Him for entrusting me with the important task of putting it together.

I would also like to dedicate this book to my two children: Jennifer and Jamie. They are my son and daughter, and both play a very important part in my life. They have watched silently in the background as I sacrificed my life for the Kingdom of God. They have encouraged me to continue when I no longer wanted to. They are really the fuel to my life because I often see their enthusiasm. I want to say to them, "Thank you for your willingness and selfless sacrifice of your mother's time."

MY DESIRE

My desire is that those who get a copy of this book will go through the deliverance process as often as needed. Deliverance must be maintained through obedience to the Word of God, consistently following Christ, reading the Word and living the Word.

CONTENTS

> *And, behold, there was a woman which had a spirit of infirmity eighteen years, and was bowed together, and could in no wise lift up herself. And when Jesus saw her, he called her to him, and said unto her, Woman, thou art loosed from thine infirmity. And he laid his hands on her: and immediately she was made straight, and glorified God.* Luke 13:11-13

This woman was said to be a daughter of Abraham, in other words, a woman of faith. She believed, and yet she was bound by her past. When Jesus saw the effort she was making, He set her free. To be freed from spiritual bondage, just as this woman, we are expected to do something, to put forth some effort, and then we can leave the deliverance to God. He is the Great Deliverer!

Introduction

Fasting and prayer should be a part of every Christian's life. I personally have experienced many benefits from fasting and prayer. When I speak of fasting, I always include praying. Fasting without prayer is like a pool without water on a hot summer day in Texas. Fasting and prayer go hand in hand and bring a sure reward of much spiritual power.

To fast means to go without food or drink for a period of time. This can be done in a group or as an individual. In Old Testament times, the people sometimes fasted for spiritual purposes in connection with religious observances (see Joel 1:14) or just to have a better relationship with God (see Ezra 8:23). Queen Esther fasted to gain favor with the king, and the Scriptures tell us that she not only made it into his inner court, but the king extended his golden scepter to her as a sign that she had obtained his favor (see Esther 4:1-3).

9

Some people fast to break bad habits. Jesus fasted for forty days and nights at the beginning of His earthly ministry (see Matthew 4:2). So, we have many different reasons to fast. With the program outlined in this book, we will be fasting with the purpose of going from the outer court to the inner court and into the presence and favor of our King, Jesus.

We never fast to bargain with God or to solicit His favor. God favors His children, and therefore a measure of favor (grace) is always extended to us. However, certain situations and circumstances require greater grace. For example, the apostles had a higher commission in the early New Testament era. This brought on them much persecution, danger, hunger, etc, and yet the Scriptures declare:

> *And with great power gave the apostles witness of the resurrection of the Lord Jesus: and great grace was upon them all.* Acts 4:33

Jesus had a very effective deliverance ministry, and different deliverances require very different measures. When the disciples could not cast a demon out of a young boy, Jesus said to them plainly, *"This kind can come forth by nothing, but by prayer and fasting"* (Mark 9:29). Likewise, in this book, we will fast with a purpose.

Introduction

My intention in writing this manual was to help you gain the skills and insight needed to present a sacrifice that is pleasing to God. We will fast for the purpose of standing in God's holy place. He said:

> *Who shall ascend into the hill of the LORD? or who shall stand in his holy place? He that hath clean hands, and a pure heart; who hath not lifted his soul unto vanity [idols], nor sworn deceitfully.*
>
> Psalm 24:3-4

With clean hands and a pure heart, we will fast for spiritual elevation, that we may see and understand the things that are being revealed by God. We want to receive the grace needed to endure and persevere throughout this fast. We want to start and also have an expected end. When we humble ourselves before Almighty God, He stands on our behalf.

> *Wherefore he saith, God resisteth the proud, but giveth grace unto the humble. Submit yourselves therefore to God. Resist the devil, and he will flee from you.*
>
> James 4:6-7

We can resist the devil only by God's grace, His unmerited favor, a strength that goes far beyond our human strength.

Also, we fast because we want to be enlightened to the things of God, His plan and His purpose for our lives. We do not want to go around any mountain more than necessary.

The apostle Paul prayed:

> *The eyes of your understanding being enlightened; that ye may know what is the hope of his calling, and what the riches of the glory of his inheritance in the saints, and what is the exceeding greatness of his power to us-ward who believe, according to the working of his mighty power.*
>
> Ephesians 1:18-19

We desire that God would divinely enable us, during this fast, to make confessions and to repent, as He brings to light the secret things in us that are unprofitable and hindrances to our spiritual elevation. As Paul wrote to the Ephesian believers:

> *That he would grant you, according to the riches of his glory, to be strengthened [that we would be divinely enabled to successfully offer an acceptable sacrifice] with might by his Spirit in the inner man [heart].*
>
> Ephesians 3:16

Introduction

Having ears to hear, may we hear, and having a heart to perceive, may we recognize and know the difference between good and evil.

Our God is a God of gods, a Lord of kings, and a Revealer of secrets (see Daniel 2:47).

> *For nothing is secret, that shall not be made manifest [revealed]; neither any thing hid, that shall not be known and come abroad [to light].* Luke 8:17

As you are obedient, God will cleanse you from secrete faults and purge you (to cause any ungodly thing to leave your heart, mind and body) with hyssop, and you will be clean. He will wash you with the water of His Word, and you will be whiter than snow. My prayer for each person going through these steps is that you would receive nothing short of deliverance from the grip of Satan and his cohorts. I pray that you will obtain a clean heart and a renewed spirit.

Join me, as together we go through the processes necessary to stand in the Holy place. May the very peace of God strengthen you and keep you through this fast and sanctify you wholly—spirit, soul and body (see 1 Thessalonians 5:23).

In Jesus' holy name,
Amen!

THE PREPARATION

Esther was a young Jewish girl who was raised by her uncle, Mordecai. Her Jewish name was Hadassah, which means "Myrtle." She was beautiful, humble and obedient, and she wore the ornament of meekness. She was numbered with other chosen women of her age who began to prepare to meet the king, hoping to be his choice for his new queen. The Bible gives us an account of some of the steps taken in this preparation:

> *Now when every maid's turn was come to go in to King Ahasuerus, after that she had been twelve months, according to the manner of the women, (for so were the days of their purifications accomplished, to wit, six months with oil of myrrh, and six months with sweet odors, and with other things for the purifying of the women).* Esther 2:12

The Preparation

As you can see, Esther's preparation was a long, drawn-out process. During that time, she had ample opportunity for complaining and murmuring. She had time to become discouraged. What happened during all that time the Bible does not tell us, but we can be sure that during her wait, Esther had to deal with some human emotions. Nevertheless, she never gave up or gave in to the thoughts of defeat or the possibility of being the first runner up and not the queen. And her perseverance paid off.

Esther rose from being an unknown Jewish girl to being queen of a mighty empire. This illustrates how God uses events and people to fulfill His promise to His chosen people. Esther is a perfect example of courage and determination for us to emulate today.

After Esther became queen, we find Uncle Mordecai one day before the king's gate with ashes on his head and his clothes torn, and he was crying with a loud voice. Esther inquired of him the reason for all of this, and her uncle made it plain to her that the lives of all the Jews in the kingdom were being threatened. He told her that she needed to go to the king with this information. Both Esther and Mordecai knew the perils of doing what he was suggesting and what processes were required. Esther answered her uncle:

All the king's servants, and the people of the king's provinces, do know, that whosoever, whether man or woman, shall come unto the king into the inner court, who is not called, there is one law of his to put him to death, except such to whom the king shall hold out the golden scepter, that he may live; but I have not been called to come in unto the king these thirty days. Esther 4:11

We, too, are faced with situations in which it is necessary for us to go before our King, our Master and Savior. Therefore, we must fight the long battle of preparation that will enable us to go into the inner court and meet with King Jesus.

As we fast, we will fast for ourselves. We will fast for cleansing, purification, humiliation and revelation. Fasting is the afflicting of the soul, which is recognized as a sacrifice. Fasting is abstaining from something, and it costs us to do that. That should not surprise us. An acceptable sacrifice unto the Lord will always cost you something.

David was ordered by the angel of the Lord he met at the threshing floor of Ornan the Jebusite to build an altar unto the Lord, and he was determined to do it—even though it would cost him something:

16

The Preparation

*And Ornan said unto David, Take it to thee, and let my lord the king do that which is good in his eyes: lo, I give thee the oxen also for burnt offerings and the threshing instruments for wood, and the wheat for the meat offering; I give it all. And king David said to Ornan, Nay; but I will verily buy it for the full price: for I will not take that which is thine for the L*ORD*, nor offer burnt offerings without cost.* 1 Chronicles 21:23-24

David refused to take the easy way out and risk the forfeiture of his blessing and the answer to his prayers. The Bible tells us that David built the required altar, and this is what happened next:

*And David built there an altar unto the L*ORD*, and offered burnt offerings and peace offerings, and called upon the L*ORD*; and he answered him from heaven by fire upon the altar of burnt offering. And the L*ORD *commanded the angel; and he put up his sword again into the sheath thereof.* 1 Chronicles 21:26-27

The Lord command the destroyer angel to put his sword back into the sheath, and it was done as He commanded.

In what area or areas of your life do you need the Almighty to intervene today? Is there a need in your life that will push you to present to God an acceptable sacrifice? We will sacrifice unto the Lord to seek mercy that we may find grace. But we must first have a determined heart and a made-up mind to see the King. As you pray, give God praise, glory, honor and thanksgiving for victory during this fast, and do it in Jesus' name.

There are different types of fasts. I will mention only two which I have done on different occasions.

One popular type of fast is what we call the Daniel Fast (see Daniel 1:8 and 11-16). This fast is often done for ten days. You can eat fruits and vegetables (cooked or raw), but no breads or meats. Drink plenty of water, but no juice or coffee. This fast is proven to sharpen your spiritual senses, enabling you to hear the voice of God more clearly. During a Daniel fast, the Scriptures explode with revelations from the heart of God.

I have also gone on several twenty-one-day Daniel fasts just before a major ministry engagement, placing my body under subjection. This is essentially dying to the flesh. The apostle Paul wrote:

The Preparation

But I keep under my body and bring it into subjection: lest that by any means, when I have preached to others, I myself should be a castaway. 1 Corinthians 9:27

Another type of fast is commonly called a Jehoshaphat Fast (see 2 Chronicles 20:1-3). Whenever we are faced with fear and/or threats from the enemy, that is the time to seek the face of God. When you are a child of God and are walking in obedience before Him and the enemy launches threats toward you, seek God's protection by engaging in a Jehoshaphat fast.

Fasting as a group is also effective. You can strengthen and encourage each other through the journey. Every form of fasting helps us to draw closer to God, so how you fast is up to you. Any type of fast is spiritually beneficial.

Some restrict the number of hours in which they take in any form of nourishment. Some take only liquids. Some eat only one meal a day during this process. Be led by God's Spirit. I have done successful twenty-one-day fasts on nothing but fruits, vegetables and water. But fasting is not the same as dieting.

Before you fast, have a plan in mind: a method and a certain time frame. Then be sure to make room for prayer and the reading of the Scriptures, always keeping your objectives uppermost in your mind.

In preparation for your fast, eat increasingly smaller portions, and drink lots of water throughout the day. Shop for the things you will need during the fast, like vegetables, fruits and juices. I usually make some homemade soups or cook up some dry beans. These are both nutritious and delicious. Determine not to take in caffeinated or carbonated drinks, energy drinks, meats, seafood, breads (nothing that contains leaven, as leaven represents sin) or sweets. Avoid fried foods, sugars and carbohydrates. Most important of all, seek the face of God.

I recommend journaling as part of your healing process. Journaling is a process proven to help trigger some suppressed negative emotions. As one begins to write down what they are thinking and feeling, the Holy Spirit assists by bringing hidden things to the surface. Journaling not only helps you to process your negative emotions; it also helps you to see how those emotions have controlled or impacted your daily life.

Some people, after they have gone through deliverance, go back and re-read their journals. Others prefer to leave the past in the past and have actually destroyed their journals. Whatever you choose to do with your journal after your victory is your choice.

Always remember, this is between you and God. You need to be honest and forthright with Him and with yourself, and what you write is not for others to read. Keep your journal in a safe place and take it out only when you want to write more in it. Then return it to that safe place. Any intrusion into this sensitive information could hinder your deliverance.

As you journal, keep in mind your desired outcome and put measures in place that will assist you in accomplishing it. For instance, during this time, go to bed early and get up early. Rising early will allow you time to pray and meditate. Each day will include a spiritual workout, and the best time for this is the morning. After your morning exercise, you will then have the power and the spiritual insight needed for the rest of a victorious day.

Why go to bed early? This will lessen the opportunity for temptations from the evil one. After dinner, when you have done the dishes and otherwise cleaned up, it will be time for Bible study, prayers, confession (a daily inventory of self, not anyone else), supplications and thanksgiving. Keep your television viewing to a minimum during this time and also avoid, as much as possible, spending time with the radio, your telephone or computer games. Social media cannot help you with this spiritual process, so avoid it when possible. Remember, this is a time of cleansing the hands and the heart. Listening to soft inspirational or worship music is the best thing you can do. Otherwise maintain your normal routines, going to work, going to school, etc. What is important is that you spend time with God.

> *But ye, beloved, building up yourselves on your most holy faith, praying in the Holy Ghost, keep yourselves in the love of God, looking for the mercy of our Lord Jesus Christ unto eternal life.*
>
> Jude 1:20-21

If you believe you can fast better with support from others, by all means get someone to fast with you. There is always strength in numbers. Share your devotional studies as much as possible, but some things will always be kept private. Get out your journals and pens, keep a box of tissues nearby, and get ready for an exciting journey.

SELF-EXAMINATION, CONFESSION AND REPENTANCE

Lord, since this is a day of self-examination,
confession and repentance, help me to see
my sinful ways as You see them.

Search me, O God, and know my heart:
try me, and know my thoughts.
Psalm 139:23

This is to be a day of self-examination, confession and repentance, the first of twenty-one days of fasting and prayer. Today, we are called to take a thorough examination of self. When we look into the person of Christ, we can see our own faults.

We can use two things as the measure or gauge: God's Word and divine revelation. We Christians often believe that we are in perfect standing with God, only to discover, through self-examination, that we have fallen short. Self-examination should be done daily, especially at the end of each day. None of us are perfect, but we are all working toward perfection in Christ Jesus.

The apostle Paul encouraged the early saints to continue striving for perfection, exhorting them:

> *Not as though I had already attained, either were already perfect: but I follow after, if that I may apprehend that for which also I am apprehended of Christ Jesus.* Philippians 3:12

The writer to the Hebrews declared that there is not one thing hidden from the eyes of the all-knowing God:

> *Neither is there any creature that is not manifest in his sight: but all things are naked and opened unto the eyes of him with whom we have to do.* Hebrews 4:13

James wrote:

> *For in many things we offend all. If any man offend not in word, the same is a perfect man, and able also to bridle the whole body.* James 3:2

Self-Examination, Confession and Repentance

Who have you offended? There is a remedy:

If we confess our sins, he is faithful and just to forgive us our sins, and to cleanse us from all unrighteousness. If we say that we have not sinned, we make him a liar, and his word is not in us. 1 John 1:9-10

He that covereth [hides] his sins shall not prosper [is under a curse], but whoso confesseth and forsaketh them shall have mercy.
Proverbs 28:13

I acknowledged my sin unto thee, and mine iniquity have I not hid. I said, I will confess my transgressions unto the Lord; and thou forgavest the iniquity of my sin. Psalm 32:5

Self-inventory, along with confession and repentance, should become a lifestyle for all Christians.

Spend as much time alone as possible today. When some personal fault or lack springs up in your spirit, humbly acknowledge it by verbalizing it to the Lord. Confession is made with the mouth, and then you repent and renounce your wrongdoing. *Renounce* means "To give up, refuse, or resign; an action showing that you have repented."

YOUR JOURNALING:

Keep your journal handy and jot down anything the Holy Spirit reveals to you today. Don't forget to return your journal to a private place where no one else can read it. This is all between you and God.

PRAYER:

Father, I want to thank You for revealing to me hidden sins in my life. I am heartily sorry for offending You and others. I confess my faults and, by faith, I believe that You have forgiven me. Help me to be mindful of my own spirit at all times, but also help me to be considerate of the next person's feelings. Help me to walk humbly before You, not thinking of or seeing myself as more than another, but keeping my mind stayed on Your great mercies.

Lord, I receive Your correction, and I receive Your rebuke. I thank You for loving me enough to chastise me, so that I will not be condemned with the world.

In Jesus' name,
Amen![1]

---

1. **Reference Scriptures**: Psalm 4:4, Lamentations 3:40, 1 Corinthians 11:28-32 and 2 Corinthians 13:5

DELIVERANCE FROM PRIDE AND ITS EFFECTS

I will walk in the spirit of humility, and the grace of God shall be upon my life.

When pride cometh, then cometh shame: but with the lowly is wisdom.
Proverbs 11:2

Pride can be both good and bad. It can be a feeling that you respect yourself and deserve to be respected by other people, but it can also be a feeling that you are more important or better than other people. It can be a feeling of happiness that you get when you or someone you know does something good or difficult, but it can also be the quality or state of being proud, having inordinate self-esteem, conceit. This type of pride causes disdainful behavior or treatment of others, and God hates it.

King Solomon had a lot to say about the spirit of pride in his proverbs. Pride will set you up, and pride will take you down. A prideful spirit is a spirit of destruction. The wife of King Ahab, Queen Jezebel by name, was a perfect picture of a prideful spirit. Although no one wants to be told that a spirit of Jezebel is operating in their lives, this spirit is real and is adamantly opposing our homes, churches and communities.

When talking about the Jezebel spirit, because we associate it with Queen Jezebel, we identify it with the female gender. But the Jezebel spirit has no gender. This spirit works through men as well as women. Both males and females are targets of Jezebel's plan to cause destruction, and Jezebel's source is always Satan.

Some people are aware of a Jezebel spirit operating in them, and they believe that it is "no big deal" and that God knows their heart, so He will excuse it. Then we have others who, out of ignorance, allow Jezebel to operate in their lives. So, let's expose some of Jezebel's character traits. Jezebel is controlling, domineering and aggressive, has no respect for authority, is loud and two-faced, is a slanderer with the tongue, a murderer, a liar, a manipulator and an intimidator, is overbearing, self-centered, stubborn, self-willed, disobedient and prideful. Jezebel hates repentance, humility and obedience (see 1 Kings 16-31).

Deliverance from Pride and Its Effects

Pride will keep you from godly behaviors, such as obeying, submitting, admitting, repenting and confessing.

When pride cometh, then cometh shame: but with the lowly is wisdom. Proverbs 11:2

Where there is pride there is contention. The attitude of pride is the origin of every quarrel and every fight. A person with pride is not able to see himself as anything but right at all times. For this person, it is impossible to be wrong about anything. If the laws say to do a certain thing, the proud person will say, "It's okay for me to do otherwise." Pride defies the law of obedience, and the fight of the proud is for first place, to be above only and to always be right. In short, pride is a self-worshiping spirit that says, "I have done all of this myself and have no need of anyone else."

Only by pride cometh contention: but with the well advised is wisdom. Proverbs 13:10

Pride is in opposition to God, and He resists the proud. A humble person, however, finds favor with God. A humble person is not proud or haughty or pretentious. Instead a humble person is meek, modest and lowly.

> *God resists the proud, but gives grace to the humble. Submit yourselves therefore to God. Resist the devil, and he will flee from you.* James 4:6-7

A proud spirit will not admit the need for God's help. A proud spirit will do all in his own strength and boast of his success. You might be thinking, "My finances are okay. The business is growing. I have a wonderful marriage and beautiful children. None of the children smokes or consumes alcohol or drugs, and all are healthy. So, what more do I need?" If this is you, stop right there and right now. Confess the sin of pride, repent and renounce it in Jesus' name. Pride is a spirit that leads to destruction.

> *A man's pride shall bring him low: but honour shall uphold the humble in spirit.*
>
> Proverbs 29:23

God has good thoughts for His children, that they would have a good end. We cannot resist the devil outside of the grace of God, and His grace abounds where there is humility. Make it a daily practice to acknowledge your dependence upon the Lord, that You need Him in every area of your life. He has given the good gifts you are enjoying.

> *Every good gift and every perfect gift is from above, and cometh down from the Father of lights, with whom is no variableness, neither shadow of turning.* James 1:17

YOUR JOURNALING:

As God reveals them to you, journal areas in your life where you have operated in the spirit of pride. Be determined to see the end of these days. Believe that you have been delivered from the spirit of pride, and humble yourself before the Lord that you may receive His grace.

PRAYER:

Father, I thank You for opening my eyes and my understanding to the spirit of pride. I acknowledge that I have [knowingly or unknowingly] operated in the spirit of pride. By operating in pride, I have offended You, I have taken Your glory, and I have trespassed against You, O Lord. Forgive me of my trespasses and cleanse me from all sins.

I renounce the works of Jezebel and her source, Satan. I humbly submit myself to You that I may receive deliverance. By faith, I now receive deliverance from this spirit of destruction.

Thank You, Father, for making me wiser and stronger, giving me insight into the importance of examining my own behaviors. Keep Your hands upon me that I may walk in the spirit of humility before You and others.

In Jesus' name,

Amen! [2]

---

2. **Reference Scriptures:** 2 Chronicles 32:24-33, Proverbs 29:23, Jeremiah 13:15-27 and Daniel 4:28-37

POSITIONING YOURSELF FOR CLEANSING

I will maintain clean hands and a pure heart.

**Who shall ascend into the
hill of the Lord? or who shall
stand in his holy place?**
Psalm 24:3

We will draw nearer to God today as we spend time in prayer and meditation.

*Draw nigh to God, and he will draw nigh to
you. Cleanse your hand, ye sinners; and purify
your hearts, ye double-mined. Be afflicted, and
mourn, and weep; let your laughter be turned to
mourning, and your joy to heaviness. Humble
yourselves in the sight of the Lord, and he shall
lift you up.*   James 4:8-10

Cleansing involves both the outward deeds and the inward thoughts. We should always have our hands and mind on the things that will glorify God. Our hands must be instruments of righteousness, always ready for the Master's use. Seeing that God knows our thoughts afar off, we should be diligent to keep those thoughts (imaginations) pure before Him. A pure heart produces pure thoughts (imaginations). If your thoughts are pure, then your motives are pure. If your motives are pure, then your actions will inevitably be pure.

For as he thinketh in his heart, so is he.
Proverbs 23:7

The mind is the gateway to the heart. If your mind is filled with evil thoughts (imaginations), then the heart is evil. If the treasures of the heart are evil, evil will proceed out of your mouth.

The Pharisees spoke evil of Jesus because He cast out an unclean spirit from a young boy. They said He was casting out demons in the name of Beelzebub. Jesus, knowing their thoughts, responded to their slanderous comments with a plain, yet profound truth in Matthew 12:34-35. One cannot speak any good if the heart is filled with evil.

Positioning Yourself for Cleansing

From the heart and through the mouth is the pathway to defilement. Nothing going into a person defiles them, but what comes out of a person is what defiles them. What are you speaking? Are you speaking good or evil? If you are speaking words that edify, encourage and give someone hope, it sounds like the treasures of your heart is good. Nevertheless, we have a lot of work to do on self within the next eighteen days.

> *Blessed is the man whom thou choosest, and causest to approach unto thee, that he may dwell in thy courts: we shall be satisfied with the goodness of thy house, even of thy holy temple.*
> Psalm 65:4

When we humbly approach Almighty God, seeking forgiveness, cleansing and purification, we acknowledge Him as being the Most Holy One. He then takes delight in transforming His children into the image of His dear Son, Jesus. God wants to purify your mind and clean your hands. The mind is the vehicle through which we serve God, and the hands are the instruments by which we serve God and others. Purification happens in God's presence, as we remain in obedience and in studying His

Word, in meditation, and under the leadership of godly instructors.

YOUR JOURNALING:

Journal your desired outcome during this time of seeking God with fasting and prayer.

PRAYER:

Lord, help me to extend my hands to You and others in righteousness and justice. Help me keep my hands clean and my heart pure before You and others. Let every word that proceeds out of my mouth and every meditation of my heart be acceptable in Your sight. I will wash my hands in innocence, so will I go about Your altar, O Lord, that I may proclaim with the voice of thanksgiving, and tell of all Your wondrous works.

Create in me a clean heart, O God, and renew a right spirit within me. Father, help me today to be better and to do better than yesterday.

In Jesus' name,
Amen![3]

---

3. **Reference Scriptures**: Psalms 19:12, 50:21-23 and 90:8, Proverbs 16:2, Jeremiah 16:17, Matthew 5:8 and 23:25-28 and Luke 11:39-40

LEARNING THE IMPORTANCE OF PRAISING GOD

I will praise Thee, O Lord.

**I will bless the Lord at all times: his
praise shall continually be in my mouth.**
Psalm 34:1

We praise the Lord because He is good. He is the Creator. He created the world, and everything therein should praise Him. If you withhold your praise, even the rocks will cry out in your place. I do not need any rocks crying out for me, because I know the Lord, and He has been good to me.

The praises of God should continually be in the mouth of every saint, and praising God is an essential part of fasting. We especially praise God for who He is in our own personal lives.

Not all saints are on the same level. Whatever level you are on, God deserves all the praise, glory and honor, for He is good, and His mercies endure forever.

This is the fourth day of the fast, and emotions are being stirred by the Holy Spirit. We will take time to thank God for the stirring. When the water gets cloudy, it lets you know there is something deep below the surface that is about to be revealed by the Light. Some of you are wrestling with fear, some with anger, some with denial, etc. It does not matter what it is; God will work it out with you (if you are willing to continue the process).

Praise the Lord for your deliverance. No one else needs to know what you were struggling with. This is between you and God. Trust Him with your faults. Not one human who walks on this earth is perfect, and we are not righteous in ourselves.

I will praise thee with my whole heart: before the gods will I sing praise unto thee. I will worship toward thy holy temple, and praise thy name for thy lovingkindness and for thy truth; for thou hast magnified thy word above all thy name.

Psalms 138:1-2

Learning the Importance of Praising God

Boldly and confidently praise the Lord with all that you are and all that you have, and the Lord will perfect that which concerns you: for His mercy endureth forever. The praises of God's people arouse Him to fight our battles. God has fought and won many great battles as His people offered praises and worship to Him.

In the Scriptures, you will read how, in Old Testament times, great kings sought God through prayer and fasting. They never set a battle in array without first setting the minister of music, the singers and those who played instruments on the frontlines. The Scriptures tell us that as they went forth, the Lord set up an ambush against the enemy. Hallelujah to the God of all battles!

YOUR JOURNALING:

Journal your emotions today, and let God reveal to you the reason for each emotion you are experiencing. Trust His promise:

Ask, and it shall be given you; seek, and ye shall find; knock, and it shall be opened unto you.
                                    Matthew 7:7

PRAYER:

Father, let my works praise You. Thank You for perfecting those things concerning me. I will praise You in the morning, I will praise You at noonday, and I will praise You in the evening. I will praise You all day long. When I feel like complaining, I will praise You. When the waters are threatening to overflow upon me, I will praise You. When the fiery trials come near me, I will praise You. When my enemies encamp around me, I will yet praise You. For You are my Rock, my Fortress, and my Strong Tower. I run to You, and I am safe.

Thank You, Lord, for helping me to acknowledge and identify my emotions. Thank You for giving me skills during this fast that will help me to manage and express my emotions more effectively. When I choose to express myself in a godly manner, I will bring glory to Your name. We have days to go before the end of this fast, but I trust and believe that You will keep me to the end.

Father, I thank You for helping me today to be better and to do better than yesterday.

In Jesus' name,
Amen! [4]

---

4. **Reference Scriptures**: 2 Chronicles 20:1-30 and Psalms 96, 98, 100, 108, 113 and 138

DAY FIVE

DELIVERANCE FROM DOUBT AND ITS EFFECTS

Doubting is dangerous.

**And they that know thy name will
put their trust in thee: for thou, LORD,
hast not forsaken them that seek thee.**
Psalm 9:10

It is the fifth day of the fast, and you may be beginning to doubt that you will make it through to the end. You are asking yourself, "Why am I doing this? I am only making myself miserable." The enemy's tactic is to bewitch you into thinking that the inner court is beyond what you can accomplish. I tell Satan and his cohorts, "In Jesus' name, get thee behind me, for it is written:

I can do all things through Christ which strengtheneth me. Philippians 4:13

He which hath begun a good work in [me] will perform it until the day of Jesus Christ. Philippians 1:6

No weapon that is formed against [me] shall prosper; and every tongue that shall rise against [me] in judgment thou shalt condemn. This is the heritage of the servants of the LORD, and their righteousness is of me, saith the LORD. Isaiah 54:17

If God be for [me], who can be against [me]? Romans 8:31

I have a goodly heritage [in God through Christ Jesus]. Psalm 16:6

Blessed are they which do hunger and thirst after righteousness: for they shall be filled. Matthew 5:6

Right now, I release the power and the anointing of God over you, in Jesus' name. You shall overcome!

Deliverance from Doubt and Its Effects

Doubt means "to be uncertain about something; to believe that something may not be true or is unlikely; to have no confidence in (someone or something); fear." Doubt is the same as unbelief and the opposite of faith.

I hear some people say, "I just cannot believe."

> *For unto us was the gospel preached, as well as unto them: but the word preached did not profit them, not being mixed with faith in them that heard it.* Hebrews 4:2

> *Faith cometh by hearing, and hearing by the word of God.* Romans 10:17

God is at work in each of us with the grace needed to believe by faith. Grace and faith are both gifts that come from God. The choice is yours to make toward salvation. You say you have faith and trust in God; then show me your works.

> *Even so faith, if it hath not works, is dead, being alone.* James 2:17

God has promised a *"rest,"* for all those who believe (see Hebrews 4:9). Some of the Israelites were overthrown in the wilderness because they operated in unbelief (see Hebrews 3:11 and 18). The promised rest is obtained through complete trust and faith in the Lord.

Fear, we know, is not a spirit or attribute of God. Rather it is of the enemy. The enemy comes to rob you of your power, which is faith, for *"without faith it is impossible to please [God]"* (Hebrews 11:6). Satan sabotages your faith and replaces it with one of his own spirits, which is fear (cowardliness).

Fear brings with it torment:

> *There is no fear in love, but perfect love casteth out fear: because fear hath torment. He that feareth is not made perfect in love.*
>
> 1 John 4:18

But God promises:

> *For God hath not given us a spirit of fear; but of power, and of love, and of sound mind.*
>
> 2 Timothy 1:7

Since God has not given us a spirit of fear, we know that this spirit is not of Him. What exactly is a spirit of fear? *Strong's* defines it as: "(Greek, *deilia*): cowardice, timidity." When a spirit of fear possesses a person, they develop a certain mindset. They may have a sense of inferiority, believing that they are somehow not good enough. They may have a sense of inadequacy, feeling incapable of doing many things. Such a mindset promotes inactivity and breeds a fear of confrontation.

But God did not leave us to the hands and plans of the enemy. God has given us the spirit of power, love and of sound mind. We have the power of the Holy Spirit working in us, to empower us to deal with any sense of inadequacy (see Ephesians 3:20-21). We have the spirit of love to help us deal with any sense of inferiority. God's love makes us confident and free from feelings of intimidation. We have a sound mind, a mind that deals with any sense of inaction. We are not confused; we have clarity, we have the ability to control ourselves, and we have the ability to comprehend.

Christians who doubt God's Word are as a double-minded man; they are unstable in all their ways. Resort to having a stable mind during this fast. *"God is not a man, that He should lie; neither the son of man, that He should repent"* (Numbers 23:19). Whose report will you believe?

We are people of faith, and we believe in Almighty God. We will not fret, but we will trust in the Lord. We make the Lord our delight, and we commit our plans to Him. Because we have trusted in the Lord, we have found a rest in Him that enables us to wait patiently for the fulfillment of His promises.

YOUR JOURNALING:

Pull out your journal and jot down areas where you are operating in unbelief. Confess it, repent of it and renounce it in Jesus' name.

PRAYER:

Father, I thank You for the truth that sets me free from the lies of Satan. I want to get to You, and You have made a way for me to enter Your presence through Christ Jesus.

Father, help me to overcome the temptation to doubt, to quit, to draw back or to become complacent, sitting in the outer court. I can and I will (with Your strength, Your help and Your sustaining love) enter Your courts. Take me to the King,

I pray in Jesus' name,
Amen! [5]

5. **Reference Scriptures:** Psalms 37:1-7 and 39-40 and 42:5-6, Proverbs 24:10, 1 Corinthians 10:1-15, Hebrews 3:7-19, 4:1-13 and 11:1-15 and James 1:5-8

LEARNING THE IMPORTANCE OF SUBMISSION

We must submit to those in authority.

Let every person be subject to the governing authorities. For there is no authority except from God [granted by His permission and sanction], and those which exist have been put in place by God.
Romans 13:1, AMP

What does it mean *to submit* or what is *submission*? *Submit* means "to come under subjection." The word *submission* comes from the Greek word *hupotasso*, which literally means "to place under, to arrange in an orderly fashion, or to assign position."

God has called us to submit to those in authority, whether we agree with them or not. For every superior, there is a subordinate, and almost every place we travel in this world requires some type of submission. We must submit both to the laws of the land and the laws of God. If we fail to do that, then we suffer the consequences of our inability to submit, and these consequences can be very serious indeed.

There are several areas where we must submit, according to the Scriptures. First, we must submit to God and His holy ordinances. We must submit to those in authority. Wives must submit to their own husband and children to their parents.

The world sees submission in a lesser, defamatory and derogatory way. But we are not children of the world. We are children of an everlasting Kingdom, whose king is the King of Light, and He requires submission.

Submission starts with respect. If you have respect for yourself first, then you will submit to others as God requires. Do you respect the person of Jesus Christ? If you do, then let us walk as He walked.

Submission is a place of purpose, protection and provision.

And Adam was not deceived, but the woman being deceived was in the transgression. 1 Timothy 2:14

48

Learning the Importance of Submission

The delegated authority of God works for us as well as for His divine purposes. First God, then the husband, then the wife and the children. God intended for the husband to do all that God requires of him for the betterment of the family.

When we are out of the order of God, we are also outside of His divine will. A lack of submission, therefore, is also evidence of pride. Pride will not allow you to be under the authority of anyone—even God Himself.

God said:

> *Submitting yourselves one to another in the fear of God.* Ephesians 5:21

> *Submit yourselves to every ordinance of man for the Lord's sake: whether it be to the king, as supreme.* 1 Peter 2:13

Accepting the knowledge of God's Word, along with God's grace helps us to walk in His way, and thereby, we are blessed. Otherwise, as the prophet Hosea tell us, we are held captive as prisoners:

> *My people are destroyed for lack of knowledge: because thou hast rejected knowledge, I will also*

reject thee, that thou shalt be no priest to me: seeing thou hast forgotten the law of thy God, I will also forget thy children. Hosea 4:6

We must submit ourselves in the same way that Jesus submitted Himself to the will of the Father:

And being found in fashion as a man, he humbled himself, and became obedient unto death, even the death of the cross. Philippians 2:8

Jesus is the perfect example of submission. The Father sent Him to earth and gave Him a purpose, and Jesus humbled Himself, recognizing the position of the Father and submitted to the Father. As a child of God, if you want to call Him Lord, then you must submit to Him and His will for your life. Jesus said:

And why call ye me, Lord, Lord, and do not the things which I say? Luke 6:46

YOUR JOURNALING:

Journal times when you refused to submit to authority and what it cost you. Consider, did you learn your lesson?

PRAYER:

Father, help me to walk in the spirit of submission. If there be any pride in me, please remove it. I understand that pride is very destructive to the person who allows it to control their life. Father, I want what You desire for my life. I know You want the best for me and You know what is best for me.

I repent for walking in pride and refusing to submit to those in authority. I also repent for behaving in a way that would cause others to stumble. Help me to do better and to be better. Help me to be a light to my family, to my community and on my job. Help me to always be mindful of my behaviors and attitudes.

Purge me of any sin that would hinder me from walking in submission. I give You my past experience and any stronghold that would have me to think that submission is an act of weakness, inferiority, lesser love or lesser value. Help me to be rid of all wrong thinking.

In Jesus' name,
Amen! [6]

6. **Reference Scriptures:** Romans 13:1-5, Ephesians 5:22-24, Galatians 5:18-25 and Philippians 4:13

DELIVERANCE FROM WRONG MOTIVES

We are commanded to maintain a pure heart.

**Keep thy heart with all diligence;
for out of it are the issues of life.**
Proverbs 4:23

What is flowing out of your heart that describes your life's issues? Is it a river of peace, words of encouragement or words that will edify the hearer? The Scriptures declare:

The heart is deceitful above all things, desperately wicked: who can know it? I the LORD search the heart, I try [test] the reins [conscience], even to give every man according to his ways, and according to the fruit of his doings.
Jeremiah 17:9-10

Deliverance from Wrong Motives

Only the Lord knows the true motives of your heart. Miriam and Aaron, being the older siblings of Moses, witnessed most of their baby brother's life. Moses was just three months old when his mother could no longer hide him from the death penalty that Pharaoh had issued against each male Hebrew child. Jochebed, the wife of Amram and mother of Miriam, Aaron and Moses, made an ark of bulrushes, daubed it with slime and pitch, put the child in it and laid the ark in the flags by the river's bank. Miriam stood afar off to witness what would be done with Moses.

When Pharaoh's daughter discovered the ark, Miriam proved brave and witty. She offered to find a Hebrew nurse for the little lad. Miriam then went and got her mother to nurse Moses, and Pharaoh's daughter paid Jochebed until Moses was weaned from the breast.

Miriam saw Moses go from the uncertainty of those Nile waters to the palace, to be raised as a prince, even as she continued her life as a maidservant in Egypt. She witnessed her brother living a life of wealth and royalty and then living on the other side of Mount Horeb, attending to his father-in-law's flock of sheep.

One could say that Moses was too spoiled, selfish and ungrateful to leave the lavish life of a prince. And yet, Hebrews records:

> *By faith Moses, when he was come to years, refused to be called the son of Pharaoh's daughter; choosing rather to suffer affliction with the people of God, than to enjoy the pleasures of sin for a season.* Hebrews 11:24-25

Miriam witnessed all the works God performed by the hands of Moses in Egypt, even the miraculous deliverance of the people traveling through the midst of the sea on dry land. The entire nation of Israel was now subjected to Moses, and God continued to affirm Moses in their presence.

Moses ordained seventy elders to assist him in the daily service. Aaron also had an important position, as spokesperson for Moses and as High Priest, but Miriam was just a prophetess and worship leader ... or so she thought.

Too often we downplay the role God has appointed for us, perhaps because we covet another's office and/or duties. Miriam became preoccupied with Moses and all his achievements and downplayed what God was doing in her own life. This preoccupation turned into covetousness, covetousness became jealousy, and jealousy became vindictiveness. Now Miriam spoke against Moses, and Aaron accompanied her with attentive ears and a supportive heart.

It is dangerous to be in the company of those who defy God-ordained leadership. Miriam's conduct encouraged rebellion, discord, disharmony, division, envy, strife and disobedience. It also revealed what was in her heart: pride, envy, resentment, jealousy and disrespect for God's anointed.

Although Moses was not present when his siblings made him the topic of criticism, God was there, and God defended Moses. Miriam's wickedness was exposed to the entire assembly. The thing she had done in secret God rewarded openly. Suddenly leprous, she had to remain outside the camp for seven days, and the result was that the children of Israel could not journey on toward the Promised Land. Your disobedience does not just affect you; it affects everyone associated with you.

Aaron was just as guilty as Miriam because he entertained the same sinful behaviors. The result was that both Aaron and Miriam died in the wilderness. Today, take time to examine *your* motives:

- Are you bad-mouthing God's chosen? And if so, why?
- Are you making innuendos about God's chosen? If so, why?
- Are you sowing peace or are you sowing discord?
- Are you praying for the brethren or just waiting for them to fall?

Notice how Moses reacted when God eventually exposed the true hearts of Miriam and Aaron. He fell to his knees in intercession for them. We, too, are commanded to pray for those who will say all manner of evil against us. Pray that their souls be converted and that they would become useful in the Kingdom of God.

When you are about to criticize someone, before you speak, remember this: the motive behind the criticism is often more important to deal with than the criticism itself.

YOUR JOURNALING:

Journal each wrong motive revealed by God. Then confess it, repent of it and renounce it. Turn from your wicked ways, before the Lord exposes you openly.

PRAYER:

Father, please help me to walk in obedience and have respect toward those in leadership positions. We know that authority is ordained by You, whether it is in the home, on the job, in the community, in the Church or in the nation. Let me reverence Your appointed people, that it may be well with me. Let this not just be lip service, but let my whole heart be in it.

Father, keep Your hand upon me, that I will always check my motives and be ready to repent when I am found lacking in pure motives.

In Jesus' name,
Amen! [7]

7. **Reference Scriptures**: 1 Samuel 16:7, Psalms 64 and 78:37, Jeremiah 17:9-10, Joel 2:13 and Matthews 5:8

DELIVERANCE FROM MURMURING AND ITS EFFECTS

I will not complain, but I will be grateful. I will give myself to thanksgiving and prayer.

Enter into his gates with thanksgiving, and into his courts with praise: be thankful unto him, and bless his name.
Psalm 100:4

Strong's defines *murmur* this way: "Hebrew: *luwn* (loon): to stop (usually overnight: to stay permanently; hence (in a bad sense) to be obstinate (especially in words, or complain): abide (all night), continue, dwell, endure, grudge, be left, lie all night etc." Murmuring is an act of unbelief, ungratefulness and disrespect.

Deliverance from Murmuring and Its Effects

And when the people complained, it displeased the Lord, and the Lord heard it; and his anger was kindled; and the fire of the Lord burnt among them and consumed them that were in the uttermost parts of the camp.

And the mixt multitude that was among them fell a lusting; and the children of Israel also wept again, and said, Who shall give us flesh to eat? We remember the fish, which we did eat in Egypt freely; the cucumbers, and the melons, and the leeks, and the onions, and the garlick: but now our soul is dried away; there is nothing at all, beside this manna, before our eyes. Numbers 11:1 and 4-6

The children of Israel were a blessed people. No other nation had a god like Jehovah. He went before them to find a suitable camp for them, and He provided all that was needed in the wilderness. When they came to the waters of Marah (bitter), they murmured against Moses, saying, *"What we shall drink?"* (Exodus 15:24). Moses prayed and God gave him the needed answer:

> *And the Lord showed him a tree, which when he had cast into the waters, the waters were made sweet.* Exodus 15:25

God gave His people sweet water, and Jesus will make the bitter things in life sweet for you too. Wherever you are planted, God will provide all your needs. Just trust and believe that God will do what He has promised.

During your wilderness season, know that God has not forgotten you. He will provide. If you are planted on a job and are not able to make ends meet, trust God to open new doors. Keep trusting Him until He does, and keep trusting Him without murmuring.

The wilderness is an appointment that all Christians must meet. The purpose of the wilderness is to prove, or test, our hearts toward God. This was one of the many methods God used in Old Testament times to prove the children of Israel.

The wilderness is a lonely place, a place of dryness, barrenness and lack of purpose. And there are certain behaviors that will keep us in the wilderness: complaining, blaming others, not taking responsibility for our own actions, being impatient, jealous of others or self-worshiping. Insisting, "I want my way" is to insure that you remain longer in the wilderness.

Remember, it is God who leads with the pillar of a cloud by day and a pillar of fire by night (see

Exodus 13:21-22). My prayer is that you will learn to trust and depend on God during your wilderness experience. Our wilderness experiences are designed to teach us how to be content and at rest, trusting God.

You may have lost your home and are now living with someone else. Praise God for providing a roof over your head. He is pleased to bless a grateful people. If you are faithful in the little things, then God has declared that He will bless you with much.

When we stop complaining about everything and begin thanking God in all things, we are showing Him gratitude and also that we have trust and confidence in Him. Murmuring and whining will keep you in the wilderness much longer than necessary.

Ask God to help you to appreciate where you are in this particular season. Isaac sowed his seed in the midst of a famine in the land, and the Scriptures tell us that he reaped that same year a great harvest.

God has promised:

While the earth remaineth, seedtime and harvest, and cold and heat, and summer and winter, and day and night shall not cease.

Genesis 8:22

Knowing what season you are in can help you endure until a change comes. Complaining has a negative impact on all who are subjected to the complaints. A Christian's words must be sweet and melodious to the hearer. Just as the children of Israel were drawn in by the mixed multitude (some among them were doubters), so we can very easily draw others to doubt Almighty God.

YOUR JOURNALING:

As God reveals them to you, journal areas in your life where you find yourself murmuring and complaining, areas like your marriage, your children, your home, your job, your church, your health, your community, etc. Confess these, then repent of them, renounce them and be thankful.

PRAYER:

Father, please forgive me for complaining when I should be thankful. Forgive me for being so selfish that I fail to see Your goodness.

Father, help me to go through my wilderness season without complaining. Help me to be grateful in all things and to enjoy the journey. Thank You for providing all that I need for the journey. There are times when I start to complain, and then I reconsider after I have begun to think on Your goodness.

Deliverance from Murmuring and Its Effects

Thank You for making the bitter things in my life sweet and also in the lives of my love ones. Thank You for making streams and rivers in the desert. Thank You for feeding me manna in the desert, for You have said that man shall not live by bread alone, but by every word that proceeds out of the mouth of God.

Jesus Christ has said, "I am the Bread of life: he that cometh to me shall never hunger; and he that believeth on me shall never thirst" (John 6:35). No more will I lust after the world or the things in it. I shall not go back to the bondage of Egypt, but I shall live and tell my children and grandchildren of Your marvelous works.

In Jesus' name,
Amen! [8]

8, **Reference Scriptures**: Psalms 34, 103, 108 and 138

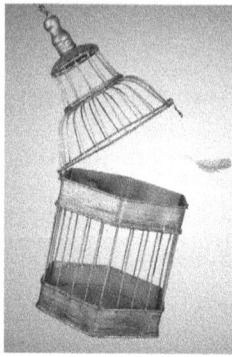

DELIVERANCE FROM STRIFE AND ITS EFFECTS

I have chosen to walk in a spirit of peace today.
I will think on things that are praiseworthy.

Blessed are the peacemakers: for they
shall be called the children of God.
Matthew 5:9

What is strife? *Strong's* defines it in this way: "Greek: *eritheia* (er-ith-i-ah) from (*er-eth-id'-zo*) to stimulate (especially to anger); provoke. Contention, wrangling; debate variance." The *Merriam-Webster Dictionary* defines it this way: "a very angry or violent disagreement between two or more people or groups. A bitter, sometimes violent conflict or dissension. Discord: lack of agreement between people, ideas, etc. lack of agreement or harmony."

God's Word says:

Deliverance from Strife and Its Effects

If there be therefore any consolation in Christ, if any comfort of love, if any fellowship of the Spirit, if any bowels [affection] and mercies [sympathy], fulfill ye my joy, that ye be likeminded, having the same love, being of one accord, of one mind. Let nothing be done through strife or vainglory [selfish ambition or conceit]; but in lowliness of mind let each esteem other better than themselves.

Philippians 2:1-3

The root cause of strife is anger. A person becomes angry after receiving an offense, and that offense ensnares them. When offense is taken, it must be dealt with in a timely and spiritual manner. First, one must repent for receiving the offense. Why repent when someone else has offended you? Because in the hidden man of the heart you are harboring unforgiveness. Forgiveness is the antiseptic that heals all offenses.

In Christ exist *consolation* (encouragement), *comfort of love* (solace furnished by love), *fellowship of the Spirit* (partaking of the Holy Spirit's life and sharing in His gifts, ministry, help values, etc.) *bowels* (of affection) *and mercies* (sympathy). We, as children of God, should have these qualities in operation at all times. Paul called for unity among the varied members of the Body of Christ.

Let us see what James has to say about strife:

What leads to strife (discord and feuds) and how do conflicts (quarrels and fighting) originate among you? Do they not arise from your sensual (worldly) desires that are ever warring in your bodily members? You are jealous and covet [what others have] and your desires go unfulfilled; [so] you become murderers. [To hate is to murder as far as your hearts are concerned.] You burn with envy and anger and are not able to obtain [the gratification, the contentment, and the happiness that you seek], so you fight and war. You do not have, because you do not ask. James 4:1-2, AMPC

In essence, James is telling us that we have issues within ourselves and when we are tired and uneasy in spirit, we tend to cause the same to happen outwardly. We are operating in worldliness and pride, and both of these behaviors are in opposition to God.

James went on to say:

For wherever there is jealousy (envy) and contention (rivalry and selfish ambition), there will also be confusion (unrest, disharmony, rebellion) and all sorts of evil and vile practices. But the wisdom from above is first of all pure (undefiled); then it is peace-loving, courteous (considerate, gentle). [It is willing to] yield to reason, full of compassion and good fruits; it is wholehearted and straightforward, impartial and unfeigned (free from doubts, wavering, and insincerity). James 3:16-17, AMPC

YOUR JOURNALING:

As the Lord reveals them to you, journal the areas in your life where there is unrest, uneasiness, disharmony, etc. Then confess them, repent of them and renounce them. Show the fruit by making restitution when it is possible.

PRAYER:

Father, I thank You for leading me to seek the wisdom that is from above, where there is no jealousy or contention. I repent of all the discord I have caused in the past (knowingly or unknowingly), and ask You to help me to make peace where I have sown discord. Help me to walk in unity and harmony, as a child of the Most High God.

As I yield my members to You, let them be used as an instrument of peace and righteousness. Let me be gentle and considerate of others, not always considering only myself. Help me to remain a faithful servant, always being aware of the condition of my spirit, and help me to have an excellent spirit.

I renounce anger, bitterness, discord, conflicts and violence, and I open myself to You, Lord, for total deliverance. I receive You, Lord, as Ruler of my heart.

In Jesus' name,

Amen! [9]

---

9. **Reference Scriptures**: Psalm 133, Acts 1:12-14 and 4:32, Ephesians 4:1-3 and Philippians 2:1-4

LEARNING THE IMPORTANCE OF TITHING

I choose to bring my tithes to the storehouse where I am being fed.

Bring ye all the tithes into the storehouse, that there may be meat in mine house, and prove me now herewith, saith the LORD of hosts, if I will not open you the windows of heaven, and pour you out a blessing, that there shall not be room enough to receive it.
Malachi 3:10

God has commanded us to give tithes, a tenth of our increase. This tenth is given to support God's work through the Church. Because this law was clearly set in the Old Testament, today some believe that tithing does not apply to New Testament times. But the Church of the Old Testament (faithful believers) still exists, although in a very different era.

In the Old Testament, they had synagogues, and in the New, we have churches and house ministries. We are still to give one tenth of all our increase. This includes money, time, talents and service.

All Christians should know, without a doubt, that all, one hundred percent of what we "own" belongs to God. He has commanded us to return ten percent of it, as a test of our devotion to Him. This tithe is to be brought to the storehouse (His Church).

> *Bring all the tithes (the whole tenth of your income) into the storehouse, that there may be food in My house, and prove Me now by it, says the LORD of hosts, if I will not open the windows of heaven for you and pour you out a blessing, that there shall not be room enough to receive it. And I will rebuke the devourer [insects and plagues] for your sakes and he shall not destroy the fruits of your ground, neither shall your vine drop its fruit before the time in the field, says the LORD of hosts. And all nations shall call you happy and blessed, for you shall be a land of delight, says the LORD of hosts.* Malachi 3:10-12, AMPC

Learning the Importance of Tithing

God has promised that in your obedience He will bless you. He will rebuke the devourer (anything that comes to devour the fruit of your labor. This includes insects, plagues, sickness, disease, etc. The prophet Haggai said this:

> *Ye have sown much, and bring in little; ye eat, but ye have not enough; ye drink, but ye are not filled with drink; ye clothe you, but there is none warm; and he that earneth wages earneth wages to put it into a bag with holes.*
>
> *Ye looked for much, and, lo, it came to little; and when ye brought it home, I did blow upon it. Why? saith the LORD of hosts. Because of mine house that is waste, and ye run every man unto his own house. Therefore the heaven over you is stayed from [refuses to give] dew, and the earth is stayed from [refuses to give] her fruit.*
>
> Haggai 1:6 and 9-10

God says that when we rob Him we are then *"cursed with a curse"* (Malachi 3:9). How do we rob God? We rob Him through disobedience, self-will, self-justification, ignorance, self-worship, unbelief, fear, pride or unfaithfulness, etc. We also rob God when, for whatever reason, we fail to pay our tithes, and that is something we just cannot afford to do. All things were made by Him and for His purpose. If He has trusted us with something, it is up to us to use it as He has directed. That begins with tithing.

What does God mean by *"cursed with a curse"?* It can mean whatever God sees fit to do to reward a rebellious and disobedient hearer of the Word.

Today churches and ministries are suffering because of the disobedience of their members to the commandment of tithing. The storehouse must have the "good news," the Gospel of Jesus Christ so that God's people would be built up, edified, encouraged, etc. Meat in the storehouse is provided to the people of God each time the doors are opened. The pastors must provide the Word, and in providing, the Word, there must be preparation. All things have an expense report tied to them.

There is a cost in money and time to keep and maintain the building, the cost of utilities and the cost for educational material (Sunday school books, etc.). Ministry is not free, and this is what God is driving home to His people. *"That there may be meat in mine house."* Therefore, worship God in your giving. Test Him and see what He will do. Would God put His name on the line and then not defend it? God forbid.

Learning the Importance of Tithing

Why would any man willingly choose cursing over blessing? Not tithing is a sin!

Let's see it one more time:

> *Will a man rob God? Yet ye have robbed me. But ye say, Wherein have we robbed thee? In tithes and offerings. Ye are cursed with a curse: for ye have robbed me, even this whole nation.*
>
> Malachi 3:8-9

Just as God remembered Caleb for his faithfulness, so shall He remember you.

> *Hebron therefore became the inheritance of Caleb the son of Jephunneh the Kenezite unto this day, because that he wholly followed the LORD God of Israel.*
>
> Joshua 14:14

YOUR JOURNALING:

Journal the ways in which you have robbed God — with your time, with your finances or with your service. Confess it, repent of it and renounce all the works of darkness (disobedience). Then, do whatever you have to do to come into obedience and be blessed.

Start paying your tithes each time you receive an increase, whether it is weekly, biweekly or monthly.

Give of your monetary goods, your time and your service. Make a conscience effort to write that check each week or every other week—whatever it may be. Refuse to let the enemy of your soul continue to rob both you and God.

PRAYER:

In Jesus' name, I break the stronghold of idolatry over my family and myself right now. I will no longer walk in the destructive footsteps of my ancestors; I will take the High Road.

I will no longer live under the curse of the spirit of inheritance. I will not rob God but will be obedient to His command of tithing. I will no longer maintain a hold on my moneybag, and the Lord will rebuke the devourer for my sake and will not destroy the fruits of my ground. Neither will my vine cast her fruit before the time in the field, as the Lord has promised.

I have a goodly heritage in Christ Jesus. I am the seed of Abraham through Christ Jesus, and I receive the blessings of Abraham. God has said that in blessing He will bless me and in multiplying, He will multiply me. I receive it.

In Jesus' name,
Amen! [10]

10. **Reference Scriptures**: Nehemiah 10:37-39 and 13:10-14 and Malachi 3:8-12

DELIVERANCE FROM ENVY AND ITS EFFECTS

I have chosen to walk in love, rejoicing with those that rejoice with a pure heart.

For we too once were foolish, disobedient, deceived, enslaved to various sinful desires and pleasures, spending and wasting our life in malice and envy, hateful, hating one another.
Titus 3:3, AMPC

Envy is "a painful or resentful awareness of another's advantages." Cain killed Abel because of envy. You have no doubt heard and read the story of Cain and Abel, the sons of Adam and Eve. Both boys were taught the importance of and the proper way to offer sacrifices to the Lord. After all, God Himself taught Adam, their father.

The first blood sacrifice occurred in the Garden of Eden after Adam sinned, and he and Eve were left naked. God made them coats of skin for a covering, and those coats of skin required the life of an animal (a sacrifice).

When it came time to offer up a sacrifice to the Lord, Abel excelled, but Cain failed:

> *And in the process of time it came to pass, that Cain brought of the fruit of the ground an offering unto the LORD. And Abel, he also brought of the firstlings of his flock and of the fat thereof: and the LORD had respect unto Abel and to his offering: but unto Cain and his offering he had not respect. And Can was very angry, and his countenance fell.* Genesis 4:3-5

Abel gave his firstlings, and the fattest of his flock, and that involved the shedding of blood. He gave his best with the best attitude in faith.

Cain, however, brought any fruit, not the first, and no animal sacrifices at all. His offerings said a lot about his attitude; they demonstrated a total lack of faith. In short, Cain made a big and careless mistake in His offerings to God.

Deliverance from Envy and Its Effects

Today Christians are to offer their lives to God, with faith, enjoined with joy, and to pick up their cross daily and follow Jesus. This is a pleasing sacrifice to God.

Cain quickly got into his emotions, by exhibiting anger and depression. Then, when God approached him with the love and counsel of a father, instead of repenting and making things right, Cain rebelled and lashed out at his brother:

> *And the LORD said unto Cain, Why art thou wroth [angry]? And why is thy countenance fallen? If thou doest well, shalt thou not be accepted? and if thou doest not well, sin lieth at the door. And unto thee shall be his desire, and thou shalt rule over him.* Genesis 4:6-7

The Lord very lovingly rebuked Cain for his behavior and told Cain what was needed to be accepted. He also warned Cain to repent so that sin would not take over his life and rule him. Instead of repenting and doing the right thing, Cain operated in pride, pride always leads to disobedience, and disobedience leads to rebellion. The result was that God rejected Cain.

As kind as God was to him, Cain refused to repent or to mend his ways. Instead, he became jealous of his brother and hated him for being blessed and accepted by God.

Cain was a tiller of the ground, and Abel was a keeper of sheep, so they worked in different places, but somehow (by some deception) Cain was able to lure his brother Abel into the fields. Once he had him there, he rose up against Abel and killed him.

> *And the LORD said unto Cain, Where is Able thy brother?*
> *And he said, I know not: am I my brother's keeper?*   Genesis 4:9

Now Cain had become a liar. Notice also his insolence and arrogance before God. His wrong behaviors led him into depravity. He entertained unhealthy emotions, and when he refused to repent, lied and answered God in this arrogant way, demonic spirits entered into him. Sin always opens the door to demonic spirits.

Some people say, "Well, that's just me," or "I'm stubborn like that." If you are one of those people, stop. Confess, repent and renounce ungodly and destructive behaviors, and close the doors to demonic attacks now.

Deliverance from Envy and Its Effects

God passed judgement upon Cain, cursing the ground for the second time, the same ground from which Cain came. This also brought a curse upon Cain's occupation. He was now cursed to fruitlessness and a lack of stability and became a vagabond in the earth.

YOUR JOURNALING:

Journal areas in your own life where you could have done better, but chose the easy, slothful way. When you sensed that you did not please God, instead of repenting, you became jealous, angry, depressed and vindictive, etc. Confess it, repent of it and renounce it.

PRAYER:

Father, please forgive me for operating in the sin of envy. You said that Your people are destroyed for lack of knowledge. I now have the knowledge of how envy can be destructive to others and to me. Help me to offer my life to You daily, as an acceptable and reasonable sacrifice. With joy and thanksgiving, I will deny myself, pick up my cross and follow You daily.

I pray that I will be conscious of my sacrifices to You, and whenever You rebuke me, I will not despise

Your chastening, but I will humbly receive it and mend my ways accordingly.

I know what Your Word says:

> *For where envying and strife is, there is confusion and every evil work.* James 3:16

I know that this kind of wisdom does not come from above, but is earthly, sensual and demonic. Help me today to be better and to do better than yesterday.

In Jesus' name,

Amen![11]

---

11. **Reference Scriptures**: Proverbs 23:17 and 27:4. Ecclesiastes 9:6, 1 Corinthians 3:3, Galatians 5:21-26 and James 3:14-16

LEARNING THE IMPORTANCE OF FORGIVENESS

*By God's grace, I will walk in forgiveness,
just as Christ has forgiven me.*

**But if ye do not forgive, neither
will your Father which is in
heaven forgive your trespasses.**
Mark 11:26

Jesus gave us a model prayer, which I believe each of us probably learned while we were small children. As a child, the easy part of that prayer for me to remember was *"give us this day our daily bread"* (Matthew 6:11). The focus of that part of the prayer was mainly on food for the belly. We were sharecroppers, and we didn't have much money, but we had lots of love. Now I know that the more important part of that model prayer is, *"And forgive us our debts, as we forgive our debtors"* (Matthew 6:12).

Debts here refers to sins (offenses), which are our moral and spiritual debt to God's righteousness. We are asking God to forgive us of the sins that we have committed before Him. In choosing to sin, we have sinned against God, and so we need His forgiveness.

There is another requirement that Jesus showed us in this prayer. In order to enjoy God's forgiveness of our sins, we must forgive those who have offended *us*.

Through the blood of Jesus Christ, we have redemption and the forgiveness of sin. Jesus Christ became the atonement for our sins, paying a debt we could not pay. Even the blood of bulls and goats and the ashes of the heifer sprinkled for the unclean was unable to sanctify us to the purifying of the flesh (see Hebrews 9:13).

Jesus Christ not only covers our sin, but He made a way for us to get back to the Father. No man comes to the Son except the Father draws him, and no man comes to the Father but by Jesus Christ.

The other element, the forgiveness of others, is also not an option; it is a command. As Christ has forgiven us, so must we forgive those who have offended us:

Learning the Importance of Forgiveness

For if ye forgive men their trespasses, your heavenly Father will also forgive you: but if ye forgive not men their trespasses, neither will your Father forgive your trespasses.

Matthew 6:14-15

Why is it so crucial that we forgive those who have offended us? Because without it, we cannot be forgiven ourselves. Some may say, "I just cannot forgive them." You're right. No man can forgive in his own strength. It must be done through the power and help of God. What a tragic decision it is when a person chooses not to accept forgiveness for their sins because they would rather hold on to some offense they have suffered at the hands of others! Because they cling to unforgiveness, their end will be as an "unforgiven."

Jesus Christ, while on the cross of Calvary, prayed for His enemies:

Father, forgive them; for they know not what they do. Luke 23:34.

He was crucified even though He had done nothing wrong. Absolutely no sin was found in him. We, however, as humans, are born in sin and shaped in iniquity. So, how can we not forgive when Jesus forgave? Can man possibly be justified over God?

When we make the choice not to forgive, we give demons the right to enter our lives. To harbor unforgiveness is a deliberate act of disobedience, and, therefore, a sin against God. And sin causes us to be separated from Him. When God is not present, then Satan and his cohorts have free reign over our lives.

Peter struggled with this issue of forgiveness:

> *Then came Peter to him, and said, Lord, how oft*
> *shall my brother sin against me, and I forgive*
> *him? till seven times?*
> *Jesus saith unto him, I say not unto thee, Until*
> *seven times: but, Until seventy times seven.*
> Matthew 18:21-22

Just as God's forgiveness of us is unlimited, unlimited forgiveness of others must characterize us, if we are to be seen as true disciples of Christ.

As we see in the parable in Matthew 18, the wicked servant asked for forgiveness from his lord, and it was granted. Then, however, he spoiled it all by going out and finding someone who owed him far less. Catching the man by the throat, he said, "Pay me." He who had just received great mercy showed no mercy at all to others. Had he so quickly forgotten how he had begged his lord to forgive him of all his debt, and it had been granted?

Soon enough, the lord heard about this wickedness and called the man in to reprimand him. "You should have showed compassion on your fellow servant, just as you received compassion from me" (see verse 33). This is what happens when we choose not to forgive those who have offended us.

Jesus concluded the teaching like this:

> *And his lord was wroth [angry], and delivered him to the tormentors, till he should pay all that was due unto him. So likewise shall my heavenly Father do also unto you, if ye from your hearts forgive not everyone his brother their trespasses.* Matthew 18:34-35

There are certain triggers that will alert you to unforgiveness in your life. If, for example, you become angry at the mention of another person's name or some certain circumstance that involved them, you have not fully forgiven. If you are maliciously doing and saying things to hurt someone, you have not forgiven. If you are spending sleepless nights waiting for God to pay that person back with evil, you

Breaking FREE

have not yet forgiven. If you cannot pray a genuine prayer of blessing on that person's behalf, you have not forgiven. Forgiveness must come from the heart; giving lip service to this matter will only prolong your tortured existence.

Tormentors will come to you in different forms, be they emotional, physical, physiological or spiritual. Your particular torment could affect your family, your children or your job. One thing is certain: tormentors will afflict you. And until you forgive, your heavenly Father will not forgive you. It's your choice. Will you choose to be forgiven or to be tormented?

YOUR JOURNALING:

In your journal, write the names of people, situations or incidents where you have not forgiven your debtors. Ask God for His help. Confess this failure, repent of it and renounce it. Then forgive, releasing every man, and following peace with all men, and holiness, without which no man shall see the Lord.

PRAYER:

Father, I come to You as humbly as I know how, seeking mercy, that I may find grace in time of need. I choose to walk as You have commanded me to walk, in love and

Learning the Importance of Forgiveness

forgiveness toward others. I rebuke the spirit of pride that would have me to operate in unforgiveness. I bind the strongman of self-worship, along with Jezebel, in Jesus' name.

Today I speak that I shall live and not die, to declare the works of the Lord. I shall live a life of abundance, through obedience, peace, joy and prosperity. Everything I touch shall prosper because I seek to please You, Lord.

I choose to walk in forgiveness. Therefore, I release all who have offended me. I bless them, praying that they may be in good health and prosper, even as their souls prosper. I accept the peace of God, and I bind the tormentors.

In Jesus' name,
Amen! [12]

12. **Reference Scriptures**: Matthew 18:21-35, Luke 17:3- 4, 2 Corinthians 2:6-11 and Colossians 3:12-14

Deliverance from Gossip and its Effects

My tongue needs healing too.

**Let your speech be always with grace,
seasoned with salt, that ye may know
how ye ought to answer every man.**
Colossians 4:6

Did you know that to gossip is a sin? If you are an acquaintance of someone who gossips, be aware of the fact that this person is also spreading your business around town. One way to discourage gossip is to excuse yourself from the conversation. Remember what happened to Aaron when he hung around his sister Miriam when she murmured against Moses, the man of God. They both died in the wilderness, death by association.

Deliverance from Gossip and its Effects

A talebearer causes great harm, damage and conflicts. Talebearers break up homes, marriages and personal and business relationships. Neighbors fight with neighbors and wreak havoc in the community.

A forward man soweth strife: and a whisperer separateth chief friends. Proverbs 16:28

He that covereth a transgression seeketh love; but he that repeateth a matter separateth the best of friends. Proverbs 17:9

He that goeth about as a talebearer revealeth secrets: therefore meddle not with him that flattereth with his lips. Proverbs 20:19

Slander comes from an evil heart:

A good man out of the good treasure of his heart bringeth forth that which is good; and an evil man out of the evil treasure of his heart bringeth forth that which is evil: for of the abundance of the heart his mouth speaketh. Luke 6:45

Slander often arises from hatred:

They compassed me about also with words of hatred; and fought against me without a cause.
Psalm 109:3

Idleness can lead to slander:

And withal they learn to be idle, wandering about from house to house; and not only idle, but tattlers also and busybodies, speaking things which they ought not. 1 Timothy 5:13

Some of us will cunningly slip into a conversation bits of personal information about someone who is not present. Even the habit of offering personal, sometimes damaging information about someone is considered cruel and malicious. Sometimes we just talk too much. Gossip is sin. Practice being quiet.

And don't be another Aaron, an active listener of things that are not pleasing to God.

YOUR JOURNALING:

Pull out your journal and write down areas of slander and gossip in your own life, as God reveals them to you. Confess them, repent of them and renounce them. Then take action. Stop slandering others or gossiping about them and stop tolerating gossip or slander in your presence.

PRAYER:

Father, as I have studied the scriptures pertaining to gossip and slander and its effects on Your people, I acknowledge that I have sinned. I confess my fault as a gossiper and a slanderer. Please forgive me. Wash me thoroughly from my iniquity and cleanse me from my sin. Create in me a clean heart and renew a right spirit within me.

Thank You, Lord, for Your Word that is a lamp unto my feet and a light unto my pathway. Let me always speak words that will build others up and not tear them down. When someone confides in me, help me to keep secret that which was entrusted to me. Help me to yield my members, especially my unruly tongue, to righteousness.

In Jesus' name,
Amen! [13]

---

13. **Reference Scriptures**: Leviticus 19:16, Psalm 50:20, Proverbs 11:13 and 26:20 and 22

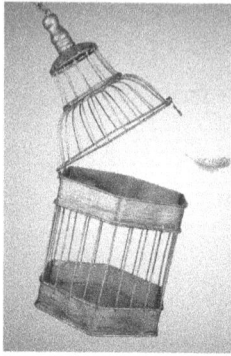

MENDING FENCES

*I admit that I have brokenness and weakness
that only God is able to heal.*

**He sent his word, and healed them, and
delivered them from their destructions.**
Psalm 107:20

During these days of fasting and praying, God has revealed to us some areas in our lives where there are breaches, brokenness and weakening. We will visit this as we follow the example of a man sometimes called the Wall (or Fence) Man. He was the prophet Nehemiah.

What do we mean by a fence? A fence is "a structure, like a wall, built outdoors, usually of wood or metal, that separates two areas and prevents people or animals from entering or leaving." Why do we call Nehemiah the Wall Man? He was the governor of Jerusalem who helped rebuild the city walls.

Mending Fences

This was a monumental task, and as Nehemiah did it, he was faced with much opposition. He kept praying to God, "O God, strengthen my hands." Enemies harassed him on every side. They threatened him and mocked him, but through prayer and perseverance, he was able to complete this amazing work.

We know that spiritual Jerusalem (the Church) has been chosen as the dwelling place for Almighty God. We, as members of the Body (the Church), are also individual dwellings of God. Therefore, when we speak of spiritual Jerusalem, we are speaking of you and me. You are the dwelling place of the Lord.

The walls of Jerusalem had been torn down, and its massive gates had been consumed with fire. The Church and her members have been through many challenging battles that have often left our walls broken down, and our gates burned and falling off their hinges. When we allow brokenness in areas which are meant to keep us secure, we then become vulnerable to attack by the enemy.

Do not be deceived. Your enemy recognizes your weak areas, and he strategically targets them. Satan is always ready to trespass what God has given us. Satan comes to steal, to kill and to destroy. God has given us walls for salvation and gates of praise.

How long will you allow the enemy entrance to your properties?

During our lifetime, we have faced situations that have caused us brokenness or weakening. Some have faced the trauma of broken homes, divorce, the death of a loved one or serious health issues. Various traumas have left us with broken links and deteriorated planks. Those damaged planks or links must be replaced. Abandonment and rejection must be replaced with acceptance and love in Christ Jesus. Anger and resentment must be replaced with forgiveness. Wounded spirits must be replaced with hope, trust and comfort.

Gates are very important to our spiritual walk with God. Christians were created to praise the Almighty. When our gates have been consumed in the fiery trials of life and have fallen off their hinges, we are suddenly left to the mercy of the enemy. As a result, some of us have lost our praise along the way and cannot seem to get it back.

Praise is an important weapon of warfare. It is in the praises that the Lord sets up an ambush against the enemy. And lost praises can be restored as we continue in pursuit of God.

In the multitude of quietness and stillness, your mind has convinced you that God has left you alone.

Mending Fences

Where there is stillness and quietness during trials, your faith is being tested. God has said that He will never leave you nor forsake you. In your pursuit of Him, praises will arouse Him, and He will return to His resting place.

Nehemiah wrote:

> *So, I came to Jerusalem, and was there three days. And I arose in the night, I and some few men with me; neither told I any man what my God had put in my heart to do at Jerusalem: neither was there any beast with me, save the beast that I rode upon. And I went out by night by the gate of the valley, even before the dragon well, and to the dung port and viewed the walls of Jerusalem, which were broken down and the gates thereof were consumed with fire.* Nehemiah 2:11-13

Take notice of how God will work with us in a secret, discrete and private manner. The Lord will meet us in a private location. For me, it is in my bedroom at night. He is not concerned about the crowd. He wants you and your undivided attention. His intentions are to show us weakened, vulnerable and broken areas in our lives that make us a target for the enemy. For some who have broken or weakened areas, God may take others with you on the journey, to assist you in rebuilding your walls and praises.

First, we must go through a thorough examination with the help of the Holy Spirit (the Fountain Gate). He will take you back in the Spirit through battles of the past (the Valley Gate). Depending on how you fare in these battles, you will sometimes be left scarred, resentful, embittered and angry with God. When God begins to show you yourself, sometimes it is important to receive counseling from a creditable deliverance minister.

Nehemiah found the walls of Jerusalem broken down and the gates consumed by fire. The prophet Isaiah tells us walls and gates are essential to our salvation. Start rebuilding.

The enemy will not be happy with you rebuilding your walls. He despises you and will come and try to laugh you to scorn, oppose you, try every way he knows to discourage you, ridicule you and mock you. He loves nothing more than to have easy access or legal rights to your life, your family, your health, your properties and your ministries. Cry out to God for help.

YOUR JOURNALING:

Where have you been made weak? Use your journal to record the area or areas, as God reveals them to you. Then, openly and confidently make your confession to God. Humbly acknowledge your need of His grace and deliverance.

Some possible areas of weakening in your life:

- Your Prayer Life
- Your Faith Walk
- Your Hope
- Your Trust
- Your Joy
- Your Peace

Allow God to walk with you as you examine your walls (fences). Examine each plank, making sure there is no deterioration, rottenness or underlying damage of any kind.

PRAYER:

Father, thank You for thoroughly examining me and revealing the things that have been broken or burned up in my life. These things are important for they make my salvation sure. Help to build up my prayer life and strengthen my faith. Restore my joy, for the joy of the Lord is my strength. I remember that all the promises in You are yea and amen.

Thank You for Jesus Christ, Who is the Hope of Glory. In You I put my trust all the day long. You will keep in perfect peace the one whose mind is stayed on You. Help me to be renewed in the spirit of my mind, putting on the new man, which after God is created in righteousness and true holiness. Help me to be anxious for nothing; but in everything by prayer and supplication with thanksgiving, make my requests known to You. And the peace of God, which passes all understanding, will keep my heart and mind.

Through Christ Jesus,
Amen! [14]

---

14. **Reference Scriptures**: Psalm 122:7-9, Isaiah 26:1-3 and 60:18

DELIVERANCE FROM DENYING JESUS AND ITS EFFECTS

*I will walk in the knowledge of God
so that I will not deny Christ.*

*My people are destroyed for lack of
knowledge: because thou hast rejected
knowledge, I will also reject thee, that
thou shalt be no priest to me: seeing
thou hast forgotten the law of thy
God, I will also forget thy children.*
Hosea 4:6

After reading the title of this day's lesson, you may be saying, "This one is easy. I haven't denied Jesus Christ." That is great. If you have never denied

Christ, then just follow along to the end of this lesson. Come along for the ride as it were.

Do you remember what happened to one of the twelve disciples whom Jesus also appointed as an apostle? His name was Peter. Jesus warned Peter that there would come a time when he would deny the Christ, the Son of the living God. Peter had been the first to acknowledge Jesus as being the Son of God. Peter even believed he was ready to die for the Lord.

> He [Jesus] saith unto them, But whom say ye that I am?
> And Simon Peter answered and said, Thou art the Christ, the Son of the living God.
> And Jesus answered and said unto him, Blessed art thou, Simon Barjona: for flesh and blood hath not revealed it unto thee, but my Father which is in heaven.   Matthew 16:15-17

Although Peter was the first of the disciples to receive revelation concerning the person of Jesus Christ, the Son of the living God, in a time of fear, distress, uncertainty and helplessness, Peter did deny Jesus. He had been one of three disciples who were under the glory cloud on the Mount of Transfiguration with the Lord Jesus. Jesus had given Peter power to tread on serpents and scorpions and over all the power of the enemy and said that nothing could hurt him. But Peter was not perfect. For one thing, he was a carnal fighter. When he cut off the ear of the servant of the high priest, Jesus had to command him to put up his sword (see Matthew 26:52).

What happened to Peter? Christians are in grave danger if and when they begin to follow Jesus Christ afar off. Sin will cause a breach in fellowship with the Lord. Where there is a breach or broken hedge, the enemy can take advantage of it. *That* is what happened to Peter (see Luke 22:54).

What caused the breach in Peter's fellowship with the Lord? There are few possibilities.

For instance, it could have been fear, Peter not knowing how to fight for his Master, the One who restored sight to the blind, caused the lame to walk, made the deaf to hear again and restored the dead back to their loved ones.

It could have been anger because Jesus did not allow Peter to fight the only way he knew and understood.

It could have been resentment because the other disciples left Peter, and only he and one other disciple went into the Judgement Hall with Jesus, to face this unique trial all alone. After all James and John had requested a top position in the Kingdom, and yet they were nowhere to be found now (see Mark 10:35-40).

Whatever the reason is for you having put distance between you and your Savior, that's what we want to deal with in this section.

How have you denied Christ?

1. When you chose not to forgive those who had offended you
2. When you chose to speak words of cursing instead of blessing
3. When you chose to pursue darkness instead of the Light
4. When you chose to murmur and complain instead of being grateful
5. When you chose to gossip and slander instead of praying for all men
6. When you chose to disobey those in authority
7. When you chose not to submit to God's ordained leadership
8. When you chose wrong over right
9. When you chose to commit fornication or adultery
10. When you chose to withhold benevolence from your mate, to get even
11. When you chose to spend your tithes on yourself and not take them to God's House
12. When you could have done good for someone but didn't because of their past

And the list goes on ...

YOUR JOURNALING:

Journal the areas where you have denied Christ and then confess them, repent of them and renounce them. When Peter realized what he had done, the Scriptures say, he *"went out, and wept bitterly"* (Luke 22:62).

PRAYER:

Father, I love You because in spite of my faults You love me more. Thank You for revealing to me the many times that I have denied You. Thank You for making things so simple that even a child can understand.

Now, Lord, help me to follow You closely. When my emotions are many, and I am not sure what to do with them, help me to stay close to You and know that You will give me wisdom at that moment of need.

Thank You for strengthening me where I have been weakened and for building me up where I have been torn down. I confess the sin of _____ _____ that causes separation, I repent of it and I ask You to forgive me. I renounce the works of Satan, and I receive Your forgiveness and, with it, my deliverance.

In Jesus' name,
Amen! [15]

15. **Reference Scriptures**: Matthews 26:35, Mark 14:66-72, Luke 9:27-28 and 22:1-62 and John 18:10-27

DELIVERANCE FROM GUILT AND SHAME AND THEIR EFFECTS

*I will accept the fact that God's
love covers my nakedness.*

**And he said, I heard thy voice in the
garden, and I was afraid, because
I was naked; and I hid myself.**
Genesis 3:10

When we hear the words *guilt* or *guilty*, we quickly think of being guilty of sin. In the beginning, Adam and Eve fell in the Garden of Eden, and because sin came in, man's conscience was no longer innocent. Then, because of that one man's willful disobedience, sin came into the world and has fallen upon every person born after Adam.

Deliverance from Guilt and Shame and Their Effects

Note Adam and Eve's reaction to sin:

> *And the eyes of them both were opened, and they knew that they were naked; and they sewed fig leaves together, and made themselves aprons. And they heard the voice of the LORD God walking in the garden in the cool of the day: and Adam and his wife hid themselves.* Genesis 3:7-8

The moment Adam and Eve, to whom God had given specific commandments, willfully disobeyed, their eyes were opened, and they knew they were naked. We call this "sin consciousness," and it cries out "GUILTY!"

Notice also how sin will cause you to look for ways to cover up your wrongdoing. This is an act of shame. So, sin is something you do that will make you carry guilt, and shame is something you will put on to cover that guilt.

Adam and Eve hid themselves because they were ashamed of their nakedness. Thank God for giving fallen humankind a conscience. When we sin, we have a built-in alarm that sounds, alerting us that we have trespassed. Just as sure as the alarm assembled in your home, your car or your business draws attention to a trespasser, so the human conscience alerts us to sin.

What happened next?

> *And the LORD God called unto Adam, and said unto him, Where art thou?*
> *And he said, I heard thy voice in the garden, and I was afraid, because I was naked; and I hid myself.*
> *Unto Adam also and to his wife did the LORD God make coats of skins and clothed them.*
> Genesis 3:9-10 and 21

Notice that God did not condemn Adam and Eve. Instead, He presented to them a question that would cause their conscience to bring them conviction.

Adam answered, "I was afraid because I was naked, and so I hid myself." Christians are not perfect. They sin, they feel guilty, and then they walk around bearing the shame, hiding themselves from the presence of God and from fellow Christians, frightened of what God or man will think of them. But, my brothers and sisters, there is a remedy for sin:

> *For God so loved the world, that he gave his only begotten Son, that whosoever believeth in him should not perish, but have everlasting life.*
> John 3:16

Deliverance from Guilt and Shame and Their Effects

Whenever you find yourself hiding from a loving God or trying to cover yourself up with some type of covering other than the blood of Jesus, you are hiding among the trees in vain and you are still naked.

The apostle John tells us to confess our sins. Proverbs records:

> *He that covereth his sins shall not prosper: but whoso confesseth and forsaketh them shall have mercy.*   Proverbs 28:13

The blood of Jesus covers our nakedness, covers our guilt and shame, and vindicates us (finds us NOT GUILTY). However, there is a condition. Paul wrote:

> *There is therefore now no condemnation to them which are in Christ Jesus, who walk not after the flesh, but after the Spirit. For the law of the Spirit of life in Christ Jesus hath made me free from the law of sin and death.*   Romans 8:1-2

YOUR JOURNALING:

Have you been hiding, feeling guilty, or carrying around shame? If so, get your journal out and make a list of those things, being very specific. Once you have finished the list, we will pray and ask God for deliverance from those things that had you bond. When we are enslaved to Satan, we cannot walk in the liberty of Christ Jesus.

PRAYER:

Father, I thank You for sending Your darling Son Jesus to become the atonement (covering) for my sins. I thank You for the effectual working power of the blood of Jesus that washes and cleanses me from all sin, iniquity and trespasses. Forgive me for my foolish acts of hiding, feeling guilty, carrying shame, being afraid of what You would think or say about me. My desire is to be pleasing to You always. I realize now that I am not perfect but am serving a perfect God, a God who provided for Himself a sacrifice to reconcile His people back unto Himself. Thank You for reconciliation and the peace made through the blood of Jesus.

Amen! [16]

---

16. **Reference Scriptures**: Genesis 3, Psalm 51:7, Isaiah 1:18 and Mark 9:3

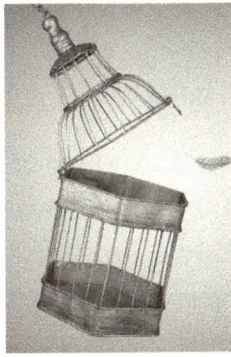

DAY SEVENTEEN

DELIVERANCE FROM REBELLION AND ITS EFFECTS

I admit that rebellion has cost me more than I was willing to pay.

For rebellion is as the sin of witchcraft, and stubbornness is as iniquity and idolatry. Because thou hast rejected the word of the LORD, he hath also rejected thee from being king.
1 Samuel 15:23

Rebellion is "opposition to one in authority or dominance, open, armed and usually unsuccessful defiance of or resistance to an established government; an instance of such defiance or resistance." Currently we are witnessing acts of rebellion throughout the world. And when there is rebellion, everyone suffers the consequences.

You have probably heard stories with tragic endings in which the act of rebellion was the root cause. Parents and/or family members sometimes will find it amusing when talking about rebellious children, rebellious teenagers or rebellious young adults. There are also rebellious adults. Such discussions are often accompanied by laughter and boastful remarks, but there is nothing funny about rebellion.

The attitude of rebellion comes from Satan, and therefore, rebellious behavior of any kind should not be taken lightly or become the subject of entertainment. Rebellion should always be dealt with as an evil spirit. That's what it is.

Anything that is like Satan is in direct opposition to God Almighty. King Saul was a prime example in the Bible.

Saul was the first king over Israel. He was the son of Kish, and one day his father's asses wandered off, and Saul went to find them. The story of Saul doesn't mention any experience that would suggest proven leadership skills. Asses or donkeys are driven according to their temperament. Everybody knows that donkeys are very stubborn animals. Therefore, because of their temperament, donkeys are handled with a stern hand. Donkeys are also loyal, hard-working animals. Still they are very stubborn, and handling them can sometime be very frustrating. In other words, one didn't require much leadership skill to lead a herd of asses.

Saul and his servant had been gone for some time and had not yet found the asses, so Saul became frustrated in his unfruitful search and recommended that they return home without the asses, lest his father would begin to worry. The servant suggested help from the prophet Samuel, and, sure enough, the prophet was able to direct them to the lost asses.

The stark reality is that Saul had no real leadership skills. One of the things required of a leader is that they first be a good follower. Saul was not, but he always had an excuse ready for his mess-ups.

Saul reacted badly under pressure, and this caused the children of Israel who followed him to react badly too. An effective leader must maintain a calm and confident demeanor at all times before the people he or she serves.

When a time of crisis came (enemies began attacking the land), Saul was nowhere to be found:

When the men of Israel saw that they were in a strait, (for the people were distressed,) then the people did hide themselves in caves, and in thickets, and in rocks, and in high places, and in pits. And some of the Hebrews went over Jordan to the land of Gad and Gilead. As for Saul, he was yet in Gilgal, and all the people followed him trembling. 1 Samuel 13:6-7

The prophet Samuel had given King Saul some clear and concise orders:

And thou shalt go down before me to Gilgal; and, behold, I will come down unto thee, to offer burnt offerings, and to sacrifice sacrifices of peace offerings: seven days shalt thou tarry, till I come to thee, and shew thee what thou shalt do. 1 Samuel 10:8

It was very clear:
1. Saul was to go to Gilgal.
2. He was to wait there seven days until Samuel arrived.
3. Once Samuel arrived, he would show Saul what to do.

But Saul was a coward, he was impatient, he was disobedient, and then he blamed others:

Deliverance from Rebellion and Its Effects

And Saul said, Because I saw that the people were scattered from me, and that thou camest not within the days appointed, and that the Philistines gathered themselves together at Michmash.   1 Samuel 13:11

So it was everyone else's fault, not Saul's. It is not uncommon for rebellious people to blame others for their rebellion.

True, it was the seventh day, and Samuel had not showed up, and it was true that the people were scattered. But did that give Saul license to usurp the priest's office by offering the sacrifice? No, this was Saul test, and he failed. And, sadly, this was just one example of his rebelliousness.

On another occasion, the Lord commanded Saul through Samuel:

Now go and smite Amalek, and utterly destroy all that they have, and spare them not; but slay both man and woman, infant and suckling, ox and sheep, camel and ass.   1 Samuel 15:3

These were simple instructions for the king and his company, but did Saul obey? Not at all.

And he took Agag the king, of the Amalekites alive, and utterly destroyed all the people with the edge of the sword. But Saul and the people spared Agag, and the best of the sheep, and of the oxen, and of the fatlings, and the lambs, and all that was good, and would not utterly destroy them: but everything that was vile and refuse, that they destroyed utterly.

1 Samuel 15:8-9

A person who is rebellious is also unteachable, prideful, refusing to submit to others, or to rules, defiant, stubborn, arrogant and self-willed. Saul's rebellion caused him to fail this second test, and now God rejected him:

And Samuel said, Hath the LORD as great delight in burnt offerings and sacrifices, as in obeying the voice of the LORD? Behold, to obey is better than sacrifice, and to hearken than the fat of rams. For rebellion is as the sin of witchcraft, and stubbornness is as iniquity and idolatry. Because thou hast rejected the word of the LORD, he hath also rejected thee from being king.

1 Samuel 15:22-23

Deliverance from Rebellion and Its Effects

It was all downhill from that point for the unrepentant king. He refused to repent and continued to point a finger of blame at others. In this way, he opened a door to more evil spirits. This is what happens when we choose the spirit of rebellion over obedience to God. The very next chapter declares:

> *But the Spirit of the LORD departed from Saul,*
> *and an evil spirit from the LORD troubled him.*
> 1 Samuel 16:14

Saul's mind was now troubled, so they sent for David (the son of Jesse) to minister to him in music. When David played, the evil spirit would leave Saul.

Before long, David became Saul's armor-bearer. Then David killed the giant Goliath, and from that point on, Saul became so jealous of him that he tried relentlessly to murder him. Imagine it! David was ministering in music to Saul, and Saul tried twice to kill him with a javelin (see 1 Samuel 18:11).

Soon Saul killed eighty-five priests of Nob because they were in league with David. Then Saul consulted with a witch or medium:

> *And when Saul saw the host of the Philistines,*
> *he was afraid, and his heart greatly trembled.*

And when Saul enquired of the LORD, the LORD answered him not, neither by dreams, nor by Urim, nor by prophets. Then said Saul unto his servants, Seek me a woman that hath a familiar spirit, that I may go to her, and enquire of her.

1 Samuel 28:5-7

The eventual fate of Saul and his sons was horrible. Saul committed suicide on the battlefield, and his armor-bearer did likewise (see 1 Samuel 31:4-6). Then, when the Philistines found Saul and his three sons dead on the battlefield, they proceeded to desecrate Saul's body:

And they cut off his head, and stripped off his armour, and sent into the land of the Philistines round about, to publish it in the house of their idols, and among the people. 1 Samuel 31:9

This short account of Saul's life gives us a picture of what happens when someone falls victim to the spirit of rebellion. Saul had acted in rebellion during his reign as king over Israel, and he and his sons reaped the consequences. When we make the choice to rebel rather than obey God, not only will we suffer; we will also put our children in judgment's way and possibly even subject them to a horrible death.

Fortunately, Jonathan, Saul's son, was a kind and gentle man. He and David made covenant, and David kept that covenant (see 2 Samuel 9).

YOUR JOURNALING:

List areas in your life where you are operating in the spirit of rebellion and stubbornness. As you pray this prayer, ask God for help. Confess, repent and renounce these spirits and receive your deliverance.

PRAYER:

Father, I repent for operating in the spirit of rebellion and stubbornness, which is as the sin of witchcraft and idolatry. I will not receive the things of Satan, and I renounce the works of darkness. I open myself to You for total deliverance from the spirit of rebellion and stubbornness.

I speak to any evil spirit that may have gained access through disobedience and rebellion, and I command you to leave my life now, in Jesus' name.

Father, I believe You have delivered me, and I am free from the bondage of rebellion and stubbornness.

In Jesus' name,
Amen! [17]

17. **Reference Scriptures**: 1 Samuel 15, 16, 18 and 31

Laying Aside the Weights

Lord, help me to leave every weight at Your feet, especially the heavy weight of worry.

Be careful for nothing; but in everything by prayer and supplication with thanksgiving let your requests be made known unto God.
Philippians 4:6

We are almost there, so keep striving for the finish line. As Jesus said, *"He that endureth to the end shall be saved"* (Matthew 10:22).

When we are faced with a challenging task, it is often toward the end of the trial that we find ourselves tripping or stumbling over something that is in our way. Sometimes we even trip over our own feet, pants or skirt, or over something left intentionally in our path. The writer of Hebrews admonished the Christian reader to set aside any and every weight that would hinder this race of salvation:

> *Wherefore seeing we also are compassed about with so great a cloud of witnesses, let us lay aside every weight, and the sin which doth so easily beset us, and let us run with patience the race that is set before us, looking unto Jesus the author and finisher of our faith.*
>
> Hebrews 12:1-2

Because I have had a great love for sports, especially track and field, I know something about the criticalness of evaluating all things in ones' control before getting onto the track.

My son Jamie is an excellent runner. He ran the 100-meter race, the 4 x 4 and the 400-meter relay. I watched him on many occasions as he prepared himself for these events.

Jamie worked on the whole man. His meditation started the night before the track meet, and his body workout had to be ongoing, if he was to meet the demand those races placed on him. He made sure he got enough rest, he ate well, he drank plenty of water and other fluids that contained electrolytes, he had no carbonated drinks or alcohol, and he did not smoke.

I also noticed how he carefully prepared and donned his gear. He wore tights, his shirt was body tight and his cleats were featherweight. Jamie made sure everything needed to run and win the race was carefully examined and prepared prior to the start of each race.

The heart of an athlete must be in what he or she is doing, whatever the sport might be. Jamie's heart preparation was an important part of his becoming a successful runner.

I began to teach my children at an early age the importance of making sure their mind was free of clutter and distractions. On many occasions, I listened to inspirational music for tranquility in my own spirit and in the home, and little did I know that Jamie was listening too. When I gave him the advice of clearing his mind with inspirational music, he had one of his favorite artists already chosen.

Paul taught:

And be renewed in the spirit of your mind.
Ephesians 4:23

Laying Aside the Weights

The body must be trained to withstand the harsh treatment encountered in competitiveness. It must be conditioned to withstand rain and snow, cold and sweltering heat and the rigors of adjusting to differing elevations.

I watched Jamie and other athletics stretching before each race. Many times they would stretch each other to the limits. Stretching will prevent the leg muscles from cramping during and after a race. Stretching is painful, but is also necessary to maintain agility. We must put our bodies under subjection.

This is exactly what the apostle Paul was saying to the saints at Corinth. We must discipline our bodies and prepare both the mind and body for physical abuse:

> *Know ye not that they which run in a race run all, but one receiveth the prize? So run, that ye may obtain. And every man that striveth for the mastery [competes for the prize] is temperate [has self-control] in all things.*
> *But I keep under [discipline] my body, and bring it into subjection.*
>
> 1 Corinthians 9:24 and 27

When we are disciplined in mind and body, we press on:

Brethren, I count not myself to have appre-hended: but this one thing I do, forgetting those things which are behind, and reaching forth unto those things which are before, I press to-ward the mark for the prize of the high calling of God in Christ Jesus. Philippians 3:13-14

"The prize of the high calling" is salvation through Christ. So, we run with a goal, and that is obtaining our eternal salvation.

Therefore, cleanse your mind, casting all your cares upon the Lord who cares for you, setting aside anxiety, depression, despair and all other emotions that tend to weigh us down. Instead, let us look unto Jesus, the Author and Finisher of our faith. One thing is sure:

And we know that all things work together for good to them that love God. Romans 8:28

Jesus asked a profound question of His followers:

And why call ye me, Lord, Lord, and do not the things which I say? Mark 6:46

When we, as Christians, operate in obedience to God's Word—both hearing it and doing it—

blessings always follow. Christians, therefore, are athletes, striving for the prize of eternal life. For this reason, we must endure rigorous training for both the mind and the body. A critical part of that training is to consume the Word of truth:

> *For length of days, and long life, and peace, shall they add to thee.*   Proverbs 3:2

> *So shalt thou find favour and good understanding in the sight of God and man.*
>   Proverbs 3:4

> *It shall be health to thy navel, and marrow to thy bones.*   Proverbs 3:8

It is now the eighteenth day of the fast, and we have experienced cleansing, purging and spiritual healing. Inclusive to this exercise, we will experience release, as in the setting aside of every weight. We often focus on the latter part of Hebrews 12:1, *"the sin that doth so easily beset,"* and fail to give enough thought and prayer to the laying aside of every weight. Both are important, because either one can impede a runner in a critical race.

YOUR JOURNALING:

Pull out your journal and document every weight in your life that God has revealed to you. After you have listed each one, then declare total release from that weight. Declare liberty in Christ Jesus. Where the Spirit of the Lord is, there is liberty, and whom the Son sets free is free indeed.

PRAYER:

Father, I thank You for being the Righteous Trainer for this race of Salvation. Help me to run with patience and endurance. Help me to be a skillful and well-built athlete, an athlete with momentum and agility.

When I am weak and discouraged and wanting to fall out of the race, set me aside and counsel me, refresh my mind, my body, my soul and my spirit with the glory of Your presence.

Forgive me for carrying things around that have become a weight and not an asset. Help me to recognize the difference between the two, and give me the grace to lay aside the things that will impede my progress.

In Jesus' name,
Amen! [18]

18, **Reference Scriptures**: Proverbs 3:4 and 8, 1 Corinthians 9:24-27, Hebrews 10:36-38 and 12:1-2, 1 Peter 1:3-9 and 5:7

LEARNING THE IMPORTANCE OF PEACE

I will abide in the peace of God.

For the kingdom of God is not meat and drink; but righteousness, and peace, and joy in the Holy Ghost.
Romans 14:17

The Lord commanded Moses to speak to Aaron and his sons and also to speak a word of blessing over the children of Israel. That blessing is very often used as a benediction. It goes like this:

The LORD bless thee, and keep thee: the LORD make his face shine upon thee, and be gracious unto thee: the LORD lift up his countenance upon thee, and give thee peace. Numbers 6:24-26

The Hebrew word translated *peace* is *shalom* (shaw-lome'), which means "safe, well, happy, and friendly; also welfare, health, prosperity, etc." In essence, it means "whole," that everything concerning you is "well" or even "perfect."

We all know that at one time we were enemies of God, but now we have been reconciled through the sacrifice of His Son, Jesus:

> *For if, when we were enemies, we were reconciled to God by the death of his Son, much more, being reconciled, we shall be saved by his life.*
>
> Romans 5:10

All things were worked out for us in Christ Jesus:

> *And, having made peace through the blood of his cross, by him to reconcile all things unto himself; by him, I say, whether they be thing in earth, or things in heaven. And you, that were sometime alienated and enemies in your mind by wicked works, yet now hath he reconciled in the body of his flesh through death, to present you holy and unblameable an unreproveable in his sight.* Colossians 1:20-22

Learning the Importance of Peace

We Christians have made peace with God and are no longer His enemies, all because of what Jesus did for us at Calvary. When we see how people are treating themselves and each other, we cannot help but wonder: is this person at peace with God? If a person has not made peace with God, they are still His enemy.

Some people seek peace in other places, things or people, only to be disappointed. Only God can give the peace that passes understanding. His is a peace that cannot be comprehended by humankind. It is a peace that surpasses tragedies, deaths, terminal illnesses, abandonment and rejection. God is not the author of confusion, but of peace. Peace starts with God. He is the Peacemaker.

Secondly, you must make peace with yourself. Someone at war with himself will always be at war with others. Christians must allow the peace of God to rule their hearts, and when they do, that peace will transcend outwardly.

The way to yield the fruit of peace is this:

1. Rejoice in the Lord always (Philippians 4:4).
2. Be gentle and patient (verse 5).
3. Be anxious for nothing (verse 6).
4. Pray about everything (verse 6).

5. Believe that you have received your request.

6. Thank Him for the answer in advance.

And the peace of God, which passeth all understanding, shall keep your hearts and minds through Christ Jesus. Philippians 4:7

The peace of God serves as a guard for the mind and heart. When we keep our thoughts (imaginations) on things that are true, pure, honest, just and lovely (verse 8), hearing and doing the Word of God, then His peace will be with us.

Make a declaration at this point to receive the peace of God. Jesus provided it for us. Our peace cost Him His life. All you have to do is exercise your freedom to choose peace over war:

Follow peace with all men, and holiness, without which no man shall see the Lord. Hebrews 12:14

Jesus prayed for His chosen, you and me, and as He prayed, He bequeathed the gift of peace. He said:

Peace I leave with you, my peace I give unto you: not as the world giveth, give I unto you.

Learning the Importance of Peace

Let not your heart be troubled, neither let it be afraid. John 14:27

YOUR JOURNALING:

Get out your journal and write down the things which keep you from the peace of God. If it is a health issue, your children, your job, your finances, your marriage or other relationships, Jesus Christ resolved it on Calvary. Remember, God is not the author of confusion or worries ... if you believe in Him. Release those burdens to the Burden Bearer. Embrace peace today and for the rest of your life, for it is a personal gift from the heavenly Father. Even as you begin to write, I release "shalom" over you now, in Jesus' name.

PRAYER:

Father, I thank You for being my peace in the midst of this troubled world. Thank You for reconciliation through Your Son, Jesus Christ. I understand that through His death, I am no longer Your enemy. We have become friends. Father, I thank You for accepting me through the works of the cross.

Now that I am at peace with You, show me how to be at peace with myself. Then I can be at peace with everyone else. I want to be a peacemaker. I want to be at peace with all men, and I want to have Your holiness, that I might one day see God.

Father, when my mind and heart would go some way contrary to Your peace, help me to know how to retrieve my thoughts (imaginations) by renewing my mind and bringing every thought under subjection to Jesus Christ.

Amen! [19]

19. **Reference Scriptures**: Judges 6:11-24, Romans 5:1, 1 Corinthians 14:33, Ephesians 2:14, and Colossians 1:20

LEARNING THE IMPORTANCE OF GRATEFULNESS

Lord, help me to be grateful in all things.

I will praise thee with my whole heart: before the gods will I sing praise unto thee. I will worship toward thy holy temple, and praise thy name for thy lovingkindness and for thy truth: for thou hast magnified thy word above all thy name.
Psalm 138:1-2

This is the twentieth day of the fast, and so there is only one more day to go. These days have been dedicated to the Lord in prayer, fasting and consecration. Your spirit should be humble and with an eagerness to submit to God. Spend this day in prayer and thanksgiving. He has given you great grace to make it this far. Therefore, an expression of gratitude would be most appropriate.

God has given some of us dreams, visions and/ or revelations, and some have received answers to prayers during this fast. As you move about this day, give Him thanks and praise for revelations and for answered prayers.

Daniel praised God for revealing to him the matter of the king. If that is your desire too, minimize your other activities today and speak less. It is harder to hear God's voice while you are talking yourself.

> *He revealeth the deep and secret things: he knoweth what is in the darkness, and the light dwelleth with him. I thank thee, and praise thee, O thou God of my fathers, who hast given me wisdom and might, and hast made known unto me now what we desired of thee.* Daniel 2:22-23

Joseph interpreted the dreams of the Pharaoh while he was still a prisoner. The prison guards escorted him to the king's presence. What Joseph said then must have startled the Pharaoh:

> *And Joseph answered Pharaoh, saying, It is not in me: God shall give Pharaoh an answer of peace.* Genesis 41:16

And, sure enough, God gave Joseph the interpretation of the Pharaoh's mysterious dreams.

Joseph had a gift of interpreting dreams and God used that gift to cause him to be elevated from the prison to the palace. In short order, Joseph became the Prime Minster of Egypt. He had been dressed in prison garb, but now he was clothed with a linen robe, had a gold chain placed about his neck and Pharaoh's own ring placed on his finger (see Genesis 41:42).

As Joseph had been in prison, clothed in chains, so were we before these twenty days of searching, cleansing and purging. For years, many of us have lived a life of captivity, with chains of negative emotions weighing us down. Now we are free to lift our head and our hands and run with unshackled feet in adoration to the God of all deliverance.

YOUR JOURNALING:

Use this time to journal, as you reflect on how far you have come since you started this deliverance process. Reflect on what God has done for you during this journey and how He has done it.

PRAYER:

Father, please forgive me, for I have sinned against You in words and in deeds. I want to say, Thank You for these twenty days of cleansing and purging, chastising, rebuke, correction and exhortation. The scales have fallen from my eyes, and I am enlightened to see as Christ sees things. My ear gates have been purged from every ungodly influence. I have been empowered to live a life of confession and repentance before You and others.

Thank You for revealing to me my many flaws and faults, teaching me to be responsible for my actions. I understand better now how to manage my emotions in a way that is healthier for my relationships and for me in general. I know that I must first receive an offense in order to be offended. I have a choice in the matter. I have learned about the importance of forgiveness—both for the one who has wronged me and for myself. I understand the importance of daily personal examination.

Learning the Importance of Gratefulness

I want to thank You, Lord, for being patient with me during these days. I feel better because I can see and hear better. I feel better because I know better. Help me today to be better and do better than yesterday, and to keep doing better every day for the rest of my life.

In Jesus' name,
Amen! [20]

20. **Reference Scriptures**: Romans 12:2, 2 Corinthians 5:17 and Philippians 4:4-8

ASK WHAT YOU WILL

*Father, You brought me through these days of
purging and cleansing, and I am grateful. I can see
You, myself and others in a different light. Thank
You for opening the eyes of my understanding.
Help me to remain in You, that walking with
You, I would be a light in this world. Father, help
me to exemplify Christ in all my situations.*

**Now it came to pass on the third day,
that Esther put on her royal apparel,
and stood in the inner court of the king's
house, over against the king's house:
and the king sat upon his royal throne
in the royal house, over against the gate
of the house. And it was so, when the
king saw Esther the queen standing in
the court, that she obtained favour in
his sight: and the king held out to Esther**

*the golden scepter that was in his hand.
So, Esther drew near, and touched the
top of the scepter. Then said the king
unto her, What wilt thou, queen Esther?
and what is thy request? it shall be even
given thee to the half of the kingdom.*
Esther 5:1-3

Esther was beautiful, both inwardly and out-wardly, and she had put on her royal apparel. She understood how important it was to prepare before meeting the king. She was still fasting when she was led of the Spirit and entered the inner courts to see him. Fasting enjoined with prayer is essential in preparing to meet with our King, and seeking favor from God requires a sacrifice. It is not that we are bargaining with God, but if God is pleased with our sacrifice, He will extend to us the golden scepter.

Now you are dressed and prepared to face the King of kings. You are robed in righteous-ness and have a crown of salvation, a gold chain around your neck and the ring of authority on your finger.

YOUR JOURNALING:

What is your petition from God today? Even half of the Kingdom is yours — if you want it. Go before your Father with childlike faith and make your request known to the Almighty. You are clothed as a child of the King, in your royal apparel, and you are a sweet odor in the nostrils of the Lord. Now make your way into the inner court, touch the tip of His scepter and receive what you need from Him. [21]

PRAYER:

My prayer is that you live a consecrated life before God, that when you enter His courts, you will receive extraordinary favor. He has extended the golden scepter to you now.

God bless you,
Jane P. McCoy

---

21. Reference Scriptures: 2 Samuel 22:34, Psalms 23, 28:7. 51 and 54:4 and Jude 1:24-25

Author Contact Page

Jane P. McCoy
Broken Wings Healing Ministries International
336 Prejean Road #107
Carencro, Louisiana 70520

Phone: 337-356-1583

Jane Ministries on Facebook @janeministries
Personal Facebook ID: Jane McCoy

www.ingramcontent.com/pod-product-compliance
Lightning Source LLC
LaVergne TN
LVHW011334080426
835513LV00006B/333